ENGAGE BRAIN
BEFORE SPEAKING

Books by Maita Floyd

Stolen Years, in my little corner of the world
(ABPA 1997 Best History/Biography Award)

Engage Brain Before Speaking

Caretakers, the Forgotten People

ENGAGE BRAIN
BEFORE SPEAKING

Maita Floyd

Manufactured in the United States of America. Published by Eskualdun Publishers, P.O. Box 50266, Phoenix, AZ 85076. Phone: (602) 893-2394, (800) 848-1192, Fax: (602) 893-9225. eskuald@azbz.com

Publisher's Cataloging in Publication

(prepared by Quality Books Inc.)

Floyd, Maita, 1924-

Engage brain before speaking / Maita Floyd

p. cm.

Preassigned LCCN: 97-90467

ISBN: 0-9620599-7-8

1. Oral communication.   I. Title.

P95.F56 1997   302.2'242
                 QBI97-40733

Edited by
Gerry Benninger

Book design and typesetting by
SageBrush Publications
Tempe, Arizona

Cover design by
Julie Hutchinson
Scottsdale, Arizona

To all the people who graciously agreed
to be interviewed and every one of us
who has been wounded with words

CONTENTS

FOREWORD

At a recent international gathering of The Compassionate Friends we spent ninety minutes with parents and siblings pouring forth their hope, doubt, pain and joy around the spiritual dimensions of their journey through loss. I was exhausted, and yet so refreshed, for the people gathered to ask became the people gathered to teach.

Exhaustion is a warning sign for me to work harder at listening and even harder at not speaking too much or with hurtful words. A mother came to see me with her sweet little girl. Her daughter was two, with flowing blond hair, glasses, and a smile that could melt even the hardest heart. I squatted down to be at eye level with her and she asked, "Where is my (deceased) brother, now?"

Shall we search textbooks, drag out the rhetoric, offer some words of wisdom from the experts on grief? It is all too easy to speak quickly when we need to listen, and especially when we really have little or nothing to say. We presume that the bereaved become a captive audience for our words and skills and we often fail to "hear" what they are really "asking", which is about *presence*.

Maita Floyd is a gutsy lady with a gentle spirit, a bristling grasp of the truth with a warmth that always leaves us feel loved and fed. *Engage Brain Before Speaking* brings the best of Floyd, coupled with the expertise of agencies, programs and individuals, in a compendium of facts, stories, insights and references to resources and assistance that enable us to listen more (which is really *saying* a whole lot) and speaking less. The book offers an encyclopedia of resources, directions and connections for the professionals who wander through this wide range of issues and wounds, and page after page of embraces for general readers who seek less about truth and more about hope.

Floyd covers a wide range of subjects — addictions, disorders, physically impaired, grief, illnesses, violence, life changes, and the language woven through it — with expertise and invitation. The book will be consulted frequently, not just read cover to cover. Wear out the book. It will keep feeding you.

By the way, the connection for that little girl, based on the tradition of faith shared in her family, led to this response. "Your brother is safe in haven, but he is always in your heart and here as we remember him and share him." Mom and daughter held hands, we hugged, and, with few words, engaged heart and hope for a moment of healing and faith. Floyd will bring those treasures to you.

The Rev. Fr. Richard B. Gilbert, M. Div., FAAGC, CPBC
Executive Director, The World Pastoral Care Center
Founding Director, Connections — Spiritual Links
Toll-free (888) 224-7685
Author of: *Responding to Grief, HeartPeace*

 # INTRODUCTION

A weight of nothing

"Tell me how much a snowflake weighs?" asked the cactus wren of the Inca dove.

"Less than nothing," she answered.

The cactus wren told her this story.

"Last winter I flew to northern Arizona. One day, I was perched on a pine tree branch when it started to snow. Not a storm, but like a dream, softly. Because I had nothing better to do, I counted the snowflakes. 3,772,345 floated down onto my branch. When the next one fell, less than nothing, the branch broke." Without another word the cactus wren flew away.

After a moment of reflection the wise Inca dove said out loud, "Like that last cold snowflake, one more unkind word can break a person's spirit."

(translated from French and adapted)

PREFACE

"Our favorite weapons are words. Because they are intangible, we think they can't do much damage."

—*Rabbi Joseph Teluskin, "Words that hurt, words that heal."*

ENGAGE BRAIN BEOFORE SPEAKING gives insight on words we use without *thinking*. Meaningless, sometimes hurtful clichés have intruded upon the lives of the people I have interviewed for this book. They come from all walks of life and have been affected by sicknesses, disabilities or traumas. Their opinions and views do not necessarily reflect the author's. Their names and those of family members' have been changed to protect privacy. My life has been touched by these interviews. Each person moved me in a very special way. I heard the hurt in their voices inflicted by lack of sensitivity, compassion and understanding from other people. These interviews are brought to you in the hope that when you meet the bereaved, the disabled, sick or disturbed, you will think before using offending clichés which cause added stress. Keep in mind that the interviewed speak from the heart and not in a literary way. I have preserved the language of each person.

We can relearn, restructure our speech, and striking unfeeling words from our response to human suffering. Our goal is to avoid being like children automatically repeating clichés without thinking. In times of stress, silent presence is important, a non-judgmental attitude, and a listening ear. Better to say nothing. Humanness is very fragile. Everyone we meet is fighting a hard battle with life's problems.

Life is worthwhile when we are attuned to people's feelings and willing to open our hearts to their suffering. It takes kindness and remembering that *we are not them*.

Henry James was asked what was the most important thing to do in life. He answered, "The first is to be kind. The second is to be kind. The third is to be kind."

Freedom allows saying anything we think, but freedom requires common decency; RESPECT from one human to another. Living together in our society requires little acts of kindness, and undying commitment to avoid hurting others.

"Freedom is not just doing and saying whatever one pleases."
—John Underwood, Miami Herald

The power of language is the power to name and maim...*cripple*...*homo*...*weirdo*...*retard*...

We all are prone to verbal cruelty. We need to understand the incredible power of words. Verbal wounds can be caused by using words carelessly and destructively. C. S. Lewis called the insensitive use of words—*verbicide*.

Words are like bullets and arrows, once released they can't be taken back.

"A spoken word flies, you won't catch it."

—*Russian proverb*

Using clichés is reciting *old* scripts, mechanical recitation without engaging brain to question what's appropriate for the present situation. Such worn out words have the power to hurt because they are inappropriate. Misused words often wound, some are devastating, and sometimes cause irreversible damage and suffering.

In many circumstances the best thing is not saying anything. Silence can't be repeated and can't hurt anyone. The world is full of critics and advice givers — a statue was never erected to them.

During our lives we meet many people. They are all significant. They deserve our attention, even if all we do is smile. Everything we do, every encounter we have touches someone in some way, even just opening a door for a stranger. A little bit stays. Nothing is lost. Words are eternal, they flow in the river of life which has no end.

Our emotions, moods, deeds expressed in *words*, influence human life and make those whom we contact either the beneficiaries or victims of our presence on earth. We are influenced by people around us and in turn influence others with our words. We should be careful not to be sources of sadness and evil.

Some people are hesitant to speak to friends about their problems, afraid that they will be belittled and given answers in a minute to a problem they have struggled with for weeks or years. Or people fear their sharing will be ignored and friends will talk quickly about other things, or tell their own problems. This reaction amounts to others making light of difficulties, as if one doesn't have the right to feel bad. Or people fear the expectation to be stronger than they are.

Often we try to cheer people up when it is not really appropriate. In a very subtle way, with empty words, we try to stop them from feeling bad. And worse tell them that we *understand*! We can't!

At the same time, we mistake friendship for a license to tell the truth. More pain has been inflicted by indiscriminate truth-telling than by lies. Many people are thoughtless, not stupid; they do not think before they speak.

If we could feel the pain we inflict on others, but we can't. We often become insensitive to the results of what we say. We all possess a *verbal arsenal* which needs to be avoided very carefully especially in time of crisis.

The solution: unlearning our use of *pat* words and acquiring the art of *engaging brain before speaking*.

People only need to be listened to even though they fumble. Stay with them, it isn't up to us to change them. Remember, it's difficult to suffer someone who has all the answers to the problems of life. What makes us think that we are *experts* on how people should react to different situations?

Sensitivity is the ability to think ahead before one says something hurtful to someone else.

Empathy is the ability to think about effect before one says something to someone else.

When people start thinking, there is HOPE for real empathy!

What will be the answer at the close of the day when we ask ourselves, "Did I hurt anyone today with words?" Have we made someone's life more bearable because we controlled our speech? If so, we can go to sleep peacefully because we *engaged brain before speaking*.

> *You call me strong*
> *You can't see how I tremble*
> *Allow me my fears*
> *I am battling strong winds in life.*
> *I need your friendship*
> *be there for me*
> *give a gentle hand*
> *give me strength*
> *to pick up the pieces.*
>
> —Maita Floyd

Part 1

ADDICTIONS

ALCOHOLISM

David is a foreman for a construction company. He is animated, a full-of-enthusiasm young man.

I have no concept of how a person can have one drink and stop. From the age of nineteen, I drank constantly. My parents used to tell me that I had a drinking problem. They would ask, "Why do you drink that much? Why don't you stop drinking?" It hurt. I'd answered them, "Because I can't." Since I attend weekly AA (Alcoholic Anonymous) meetings I know why I couldn't stop.

My older brother wouldn't talk to me because I am an alcoholic. My ex-wife used to resent my regular attendance at AA meetings, but know I need the group support to live one day at a time. People have a hard time understanding that alcoholism is a disease because they think that it is a matter of *willpower*. I was so tired of hearing,

"It's only a matter of *willpower*. That's all!"

I have been sober more than three years, people keep throwing the past at me. "You used to do this, do that." It is very annoying, like a monkey on my back. I know what I am doing now, and my outlook on life has changed. It is taking me a while to rebuild my trust in people, especially the closest to me.

I've often been asked, "How many DUIs (driving under the influence) have you had?" When I answer none, people look surprised. They add, "You can't be an alcoholic." People have a tendency to stereotype us.

Since I am in AA people feel uncomfortable drinking in front of me. They walk on eggs. It's what they don't say, their attitude — which hurts the most.

"Always be a little kinder than necessary."

—*James M. Barrie*

ALCOHOLISM

In his mid-forties, Sam is a bank manager. He came up through the ranks with hard work and perseverance.

What bothers me the most is when a person asks me if I am a *real* alcoholic. I don't know what they mean. In the alcoholic world, we call people who don't drink, straight people. They make such statements as,

If only they would use their willpower!
They come from such a nice family!
They are so intelligent!
I know their parents taught them better!

Such comments are indicative of people who have no knowledge about what goes on in the mind and life of an alcoholic whether sober or drunk.

In dealing with people who are without knowledge about the alcoholic world, I am always a little disturbed when they say, "Why can't you have one drink. Just a glass of wine to be sociable. It can't possibly hurt you."

They can create such untold damage with that *just one drink*. One never hears a person insisting that a diabetic have *just one piece of cake*. It won't hurt you. No, they would worry about causing a diabetic coma. It is beyond the mind how to tell them.

A game played with alcoholics is the *if* game.

If my husband would just pay more attention to me...

If my husband would just take the children for a walk, a ball game or a drive...

If my husband would just...

and it always ends with, everything would be alright if he wouldn't drink anymore! These are dreams, fantasy worlds in which people live that are not reality.

Society has yet to realize the benefits of the application of the twelve steps of Alcoholic Anonymous to all phases of life.

One of my first experiences at an AA meeting was listening to and reading the twelve steps of recovery. A couple years later, the first step finally jumped at me, but it was rewritten like this: admitted I was powerless over alcohol and that my wife was unmanageable. That's the cunningness of alcoholics — to transport just a little bit, making it into such an entirely different phenomenon.

"Be not angry that you can't make others as you wish them since you can't make yourself as you wish to be."

—*Thomas A'Kempis*

☎ Alcoholic Anonymous   (212) 685-1110
☎ Al-Anon (Family members
   of alcoholics)   (800) 356-9996

DRUG
ADDICTION

J osh agreed to be interviewed even though it was going to be painful, hoping that his story would open people's eyes about drug addiction.

I was clean for five years. I went back to my home state and within a few weeks I was a daily user. Several years later my father died. It was very hard because by that time I was dealing drugs. I couldn't deal with his death, I wasn't ready for it. I started buying and selling in large quantities. Crystal was my drug of *choice*. My addiction got worse. I drifted from the family because nobody could understand what I was going through. It hurt me a great deal. Then I got busted with ten grams of crystal, paraphernalia and possession of a gun. My sentence was thirty days in the Arizona Maricopa County jail called tent city, (prisoners live in tents), five years probation, $1500 fine and 360 hours of community service. If I violate my probation I'm looking at four to eight years of prison time.

For the longest time I didn't care, and come up dirty a bunch of times for drugs. When you are on probation you can't do drugs. I didn't care about the community service, I didn't pay my fine or fees and I had ten dirty UIs (under the influence of drugs) in one year. My probation officer was able to convince the judge to give me extensive probation which is house arrest. You can go to work, but that's it. I have been on it three months, it's rough. I can't see my girlfriend because she had used drugs with me. She has been clean longer than I have, and is going through a drug counseling program.

I have a hard time trusting. It's very difficult. Ever since I was a child my parents didn't pay attention to me because my father had a gambling problem and alcohol addiction. He was always on the fast lane. He worked sixteen hours a day then went to the races, came home get a few hours of sleep and went back to work. Dad did that for seven days a week for more than twenty years. My mother was co-dependent. It has been a rough life. I have come a long way in the past year. I've had a full time job for more than a year. I work for a company that lays lines underground, and just got promoted to assistant foreman. I work more than forty hours a week. I had an addiction, might as well be a workaholic and make money. Everybody tells me that I am doing great, I have a job. My bosses trust me.

I now do my community service. I have a surveillance officer, pay my fees. I am really powerless. He was really tough on me for the first month. He can tell you that I have come a long way. Sometimes I am called on the job at midnight, two o'clock in the morning—I am there. I am really starting to come around.

Although I can't see my girlfriend, she gives me all the support I need, the most I ever had in my whole life. For a long time I didn't trust her. I am starting to now. At times I don't, my mind is playing tricks.

The biggest part is *nobody* knows what you go through, how hard it is. After I got off the stuff, I couldn't get out of bed for weeks. I was at my mom's. I'd get up from the couch to go to the bathroom and back to the couch where I slept. That was the most energy I had. I would stop for one week, then use again, then be clean for thirty days, then forty days. I have never made it this far since 1988. Gets easier? I know that if I use again I am going to prison. I almost needed my back against the wall.

It helps tremendously that I am going through an attachment/holding program.

My regular attendance at NA (Narcotic Anonymous) meetings has given me new hope. I have a fear of being alone. It's hard without my girlfriend. Can't have drugs, or see my family.

Me and mom talk now. We're getting closer, still I don't trust her. For too many years she put me down. She would praise me for ten seconds then cut me down for thirty minutes. It was real hard. When I was a teenager my mom would ground me all the time for smoking, bad grades, would never give me any praise or credit. If I got a C it wasn't good enough.

My brother is president of a large company in the Midwest, my other brother owns a very expensive home. Here I am, just like this, but finally I am happy.

Now I don't care about what people think or say about me.

Before I stopped using, the hurtful cliché was, "You can stop," but you can't see that when you are using. The addiction gets a hold of you so strongly. I've even had a family member tell me, "I knew that you were going use it again." It's bad enough to have an addiction without people pushing you down further instead of being supportive.

I went to see a doctor to be tested (urine test). I told him that I had been clean for 104 days! He said, "That's not long enough." Previously I had never made it for more than ninety days. It was not bad enough that he added, "You can't be with your girlfriend you are not good for each other." This doctor is the perfect example. He could have said, "That's wonderful, keep it up." I need people to tell me it's wonderful to keep on going. My therapist recognizes that I am doing so good, he gives me a lot of support.

There is no way people can know what you are going through. Lot of times they don't praise you, that's the biggest thing, they don't praise you. They only want facts, they are not addicts. Drugs take a lot out of you, I LOVE it for the *five* minutes I am on then I *hate* it.

Supportive friends usually say, "You can make it once you stop." But, others say, "Let's party one more time before you stop." The last time I thought I could do that. For a while, I thought I was controlling *it*. Use one day during the week-end, before too long it was two nights then full time. I couldn't get off it.

My addiction is I want a fast one (life) like my father. I didn't like people, isolated myself and now I am *being* isolated. My girlfriend is a recovering addict, that's even worse. If she uses I will have to say goodbye. I need to hold on to whatever I have.

At NA (Narcotics Anonymous) I have a wonderful sponsor who has been clean for five years. I used to work with him. Great people there. We even celebrate if someone is clean *four* days. Some have no jobs, ten cents in their pockets, all the stuff in the house is gone because it was traded for drugs. People don't understand.

My father and I were buddies in our addiction. After he died my mother kept on saying, "I am alone. Why can't *you* stand being alone?" My girlfriend and I have to realize that we must stay away from the same people, same crowds. Letting go is the hardest thing to do. From my girlfriend I want to be loved. It's not sex, it's companionship. Just to be held. I was not held when I was a kid.

I am starting to like myself, sometimes I didn't because of past mistakes. I want to trust people, but there are times I still can't. I am getting there, but it's hard. I used to think that the world was against me. Now I live on love addiction; I am a love addict. I look forward seeing my girlfriend again, at times I have to back away.

I went through three marriages. I was married when I was a teenager, it lasted two years. The second lasted almost eleven years, and I have been divorced since 1990 from my third wife.

People who have never smoked, been hooked on drugs or alcohol cannot understand the agony of withdrawal.

Most people with addictions are told, "It's a matter of will power." Easy to judge. You aren't walking in my moccasins.

"To fall down you manage alone, but it takes friendly hands to get up."

—*Yiddish proverb*

☎ NARCOTICS ANONYMOUS   (800) 352-3792

FOOD ADDICTION

Naomi is a striking blonde with a figure that makes men's heads turn. It is hard to believe that at one time she weighed more than 300 pounds. She regularly attends OA (Overeater Anonymous) meetings, a twelve-step program for eating disorders.

I was very aware from a very young age that I was the heaviest person around. The worst, worst hurtful thing was that I was different and always picked on. There were not many fat kids around.

Hurtful names and comments have stuck with me like, "Fatty, fatty. Two by four."

"You are so fat that you can't walk or play."
"We are going biking, you can't come. You might get all tired out. You should stay home."
"We are going ice skating, you better not come."

"Aren't you ready to lose you baby fat yet?"
"Do you know how unhealthy it is to be fat?"
"You are so pretty. Why don't you lose weight?"
"Why don't you stop eating!"
"You have to go on a diet."

Devastating!
My earliest recollections of being hurt are from grammar school. Many teachers thought that since I was fat my brain couldn't function like the other students. When I was a kid an aunt used to repeat, "You've got to lose weight, you've got to lose weight." The natural reaction was to balk, fight back and do the opposite.

I couldn't go shopping for clothes in a regular store with the other kids. I had to go to Lane Bryant (store for large sizes only). Even there, saleswomen would invariably say, "I don't think that we have your size" because I was a child, or "You wouldn't look well in this dress." I felt bad that I couldn't dress like other children.

Mothers would warn their children, "If you keep eating you are going to look like Naomi. Look how fat she is!"

As I started growing up and maturing I was always being bribed, "I will buy you this or that if you lose weight." It created stress and actually worked in reverse.

When I weighed 300 pounds in a grocery store a little girl yelled, "That lady works in a circus." I was so embarrassed that I could have died. A lot of hurtful things are said by children. It's their parents' fault, they should correct them.

I was afraid of going out, because someone might look and make remarks. I cringed when I heard that my head looked like a watermelon. Also I was asked if I bought my clothes at the tentmaker.

When I had an operation, my doctor was kind. He said, "It would be easier if you were thinner!" How nice to have someone refer to your weight without hurtful clichés.

I had a girlfriend whose five-year old was a brat. One day she came over. As soon as they walked in he looked at me and said, "Are you ever fat!" He then kicked me in the leg repeating his nasty remark. I asked my friend, "Aren't you going to reprimand him? Why aren't you teaching him manners?" She answered, "It's cute!" Needless to say that my close friend is no longer my friend. It hurt so bad.

It was devastating to go to the community pool. At 240 pounds I was the heaviest person there. When I went to the beach I heard such comments, "She looks like a beached whale!" It was how I actually felt.

I applied for different jobs, and know I didn't get some of them because I was overweight. The standard answer was, "Sorry, we can't use you."

One Christmas, a candy store was handing out free candy. A woman approached me saying, "You don't need it. I'll take yours." I was stunned. Why should she assume that the candy was for me. I was there for my children. Shopping for my daughter in a department store junior petite section a clerk who had seen me in the large sizes area said, "You can't wear these sizes." How insulting!

In restaurants people snickered and glanced at my plate to see what I was eating. It was horrible and even more horrible when they used their body language. People would puff up their faces and imitate the way I walked.

When I was involved with various charities I would attend banquets. My friends would choose my menu, knowing better than I what I should eat. All for my benefit!

I don't care if they are adults or children, if you are different, they stare. People would look at me as if I were from outer space. Wherever I went, I'd see them whispering. The whispers grew so loud in my mind. Why can't people like you for what you are and not what you look like.

Some of my friends were embarrassed to be seen with me. When I was the heaviest, I was called *big Bubbles*. It was a hurtful name. I just wanted to be called by my name, Naomi. I even was asked if I had a thyroid problem. It is so awful to be stared at and criticized. My fat was becoming their problem.

It's hard to lose weight when the only thing you love is *food*. It was my whole nurturing in my life. A lot of things were ruined in my life on account of my weight. I am fifty-five and no longer fat but still feel the pain.

We live in a *THIN* world. Being thin doesn't make you happy. Happiness comes from within. I have serenity knowing why I ate. People don't realize the hurt they inflict. Name calling is the worst thing a *fat* person can go through, spiteful, uncaring clichés and words. People don't mind their own business.

"What wisdom can you find greater than kindness?"

—*Jean Jacques Rousseau*

☎ Overeaters Anonymous
　 World Service　　　　　　　　(505) 891-2664

Part 2

DISORDERS

EPILEPSY

Liz is a quiet eleven years old. She has naturally wavy, dark brown hair. She is an excellent student, among the top three in her class. Liz has been seizure-free for more than a year. The interview was conducted with her mother.

It was hard when Liz had her first seizure at five years old. She doesn't remember much about it. At that time epilepsy was ruled out. I was supposedly a neurotic mother and being the middle child, we were told that Liz was seeking attention. From the start, we made it a positive experience and would not let it interfere with her life. People with epilepsy are far more disadvantaged by other people's attitudes than by their disorder.

One day Liz and I went shopping in a department store. It was a time that her medication was being changed. She had a seizure, fell down and got sick to her stomach. Right away a crowd of people formed, watching the whole thing. I asked someone to give me some tissues to clean her. The store manager came running, afraid that Liz had slipped and I would sue the store. He was real nice, brought some soda and crackers to settle her stomach. Later as we continued shopping, people pointed, whispered...that's the one. The shoppers' attitude was devastating for Liz.

I had a very bad experience with one man who was very curt and hurtful. He said, "I hope Liz never has a seizure in front of my kids because when I was in grade school a kid had one. It was scary. He was retarded, really retarded. I don't want my children to have the same experience. My wife and I don't want our kids to get a bad impression of Liz." That hurt a lot.

Parents don't want Liz to spend the night at their house. They are afraid that she might have a seizure even though she is now seizure free. She also is not invited to parties. It is very hard on her. She even has been called *weirdo*. Is there any *weird* ailment?

When I tell some people about Liz's epilepsy they start crying like Liz was going to die or something very bad would happen to her. It upsets me! When I told my sister that Liz had epilepsy she said, "Maybe there is a reason. Maybe she can use this to help other people. She is chosen!"

We have been very up front about it, teachers have been very supportive. I try not to use it as a crutch. I didn't want to say, "It might happen. She is a little bit tired, not quite herself." I don't want epilepsy used as the reason if she doesn't do well, but still the medication may be a

34

factor when she is unable to perform. The school needs
to know what's wrong with children.

When my husband and I agreed to let her appear on
television many people told us, "Why do you want everyone to know?" She was selected for the appearance on a
program on neurological disorders. Epilepsy should not
stay in the closet. It would help children with epilepsy,
their parents and educate the viewers against the stigma.

I asked a friend, "What would you do if it was your
child?" Without hesitation she answered, "I absolutely
wouldn't let him do it." The word *epilepsy* has an effect
on people which is vastly different than if she had cancer,
then it would be okay to talk about it on television.[1]

We joined our state Epilepsy Society so Liz would meet
other children at support groups with whom she could
identify.

Another cliché, "Big deal...so you have epilepsy...live
with it."

---

1   **Author's note:** A Dallas radio talk show host told a sick joke,
    "Seizure salad." After receiving several letters of disgust his
    answer was, "If you are a human being, and you're breathing,
    you get no respect around here. It's the American way!"

    A listener wrote, "You don't represent the American way, you
    defile it."

    It seems that our society thrives on controversy, attacking
    people who can't defend themselves. Epilepsy still has a very
    strong stigma, let's not make it worse for our children and adults
    who have this disorder. It is people like that commentator who
    teach others to lose a basic value — RESPECT.

It's devastating, after a seizure, to be called drunk or a weirdo. Should any disorder be called weird?

"Preserve us from the destructive power of words! There are words which can separate hearts sooner than sharp swords. There are words whose sting can remain through a whole life.

—*Mary Botham Howitt*

☎ **Epilepsy Society of America**   **(800) EFA-1000**

CEREBRAL PALSY

Bob *is a tall young man with greenish eyes. He has a wonderful sense of humor. He lives with his parents.*

I was born with cerebral palsy. The cause it not known. Ever since people have made fun of me, making me feel like an outcast. One day my Dad and I were in a parking lot. A man passing by said, "You are handicapped." I answered, "Oh! Am I? I am not handicapped. I am normal like you."

My Mom says that when I was little religious people wanted to come and cure me. If you are religious, that's fine. I don't want to offend, but I am healthy. I have a job and have very cool parents. I don't need anything else. If there is a God out there, he put me on this earth to explain to people that everybody is different.

Before I went to high school for the blind I attended a regular school. When I sat next to other kids some would say, "Don't touch me," maybe because they thought they would become like me. They said stupid stuff like calling me *retard*. It has been like that ever since I can remember. Life is hard.

I am legally blind. I can see, but it takes my brain and my eyes longer to process the picture. People can't believe what blind people can do.

One day I took a box of Kleenex to scratch my back. One kid said, "What is he doing?" The teacher answered, "He is scratching his back." That was the only way I could reach that spot with one good arm. I scratch places I can't reach against a table, wall, anything that will do the job.

When I attended the high school for the blind it was easier because there were young people like me. I felt at home. I would take a bus to get there. One day at the bus stop a woman with a baby, a carriage and a bag of groceries was also waiting. I wondered how she would manage to get on. I told her that I would take the groceries. When I boarded the bus, the driver told me, "You are cool!"

At work as a cashier in a chain clothing store, customers would ask, "Did you have a stroke?"

"No, I was born like this," is my standard answer.

I use a magnifying glass to read when the print is real small. I hate it when people tell me, "Why don't you wear glasses?" They wouldn't understand like you do. Why do I have to explain when I do things differently from other people?

Kids will come to me and ask, "What's wrong with your arm?" My answer is, "I am like a TV. My brain is the reception box. Between my brain and my arm there is a wire loose. My arm can't get the message like yours does. That's why it stays bent." When I explain, they look at me and say okay. Kids understand, they have a more open mind than we adults do. We don't give kids enough credit. I have been asked weird questions, like, "How do you put your shoes on? How do you dress?" The answer is one leg at the time... It is amazing, like I am an alien from a different planet.

Sometimes at work a person will go to another cashier saying, "He is really slow."

I couldn't believe it. I would like to see that person do this job. It took me a long time to get adjusted to do things with one hand. One day a customer said to a co-worker that he couldn't understand why the store employed handicapped persons. It took all his willpower not to punch the man. It blew his mind away. To my co-workers I am not handicapped, I am normal. They always side with me, stick up for me. My employers treat me like there is nothing wrong with me. My regular customers, like you, treat me as a cashier — period. Sometimes we get off-the-wall people. My mother and I went shopping, the cashier was having a hard time bagging our purchases in a plastic bag. I told him, "I understand, those bags can be a pain with one or two arms." I can relate to people who have the same kind of job as mine. I have my own way of doing things. For example if people buy books, I stand them up and slide the bag over them.

When someone comes to pay for their purchases with a broken arm, I can tell them that I know what it is to have only one workable arm. I can joke with people. A woman in a wheelchair comes in regularly. I tease her, sometimes telling her, "Don't run any red lights." She laughs. What is wrong with the world is that not enough people wonder if others need some help. Life is funny! Life is hard for everyone.

I have had more pain from people who have made fun of me. They will for the rest of my life. My scars are for life. At times I forget about them, but they are still there. I don't care what they think. People who know me treat me like everybody else. I wish that people who make fun of the physically challenged could walk in our shoes for one day. Being made fun of is like being punched, it hurts. Ridicule gives us mental scars that no one can ever see. Many are cruel. People should use their words wisely, open their minds.

I don't want people to treat me like an outsider. That bugs me. I am like everybody else inside, same thoughts and feelings as anybody else. I enjoy looking at pretty women, like some things that others like. I believe one thing that will never die is discrimination against the handicapped. In a way everybody in the world is handicapped. I might be able to do something that you can't do very good.

When I wake up I feel normal, but sometimes I wonder if some day people will stop asking, "What's wrong with you?" Nothing is wrong with me, I want to say, what's wrong with YOU?

My father, a supervisor in a small plant asked a partly deaf man to do a chore. He complained to Dad that the job was too difficult with his handicap. My father answered him, "No, my son is physically challenged, has cerebral palsy. He is a better worker than you are. He doesn't use his handicap to get out of doing his job."

When I go to other stores people look at me because of the way I walk, "What's wrong with him?" It's funny, I love watching people a lot, especially at work. The way they look at me. My mind says, "I know what you are thinking. I am just like you, man." It hurts. We are all different in our own way. I feel the whole world has to wake up.

How come a famous star like Christopher Reeve who got hurt in a riding accident, they want him to talk to the world and say, "This is what the physically challenged need. What can I do for you? What can we do to make your life and others better?" It shouldn't take a famous person to hurt themselves for the world to see what's out there. Let's go out to speak to the general public, people like me who are physically challenged. Who cared before that?

I have touched some people because I have not let my cerebral palsy stop me from leading a normal life. Like the little train, "I could."

Some day I would like to go sky diving. I like rock music, but also classical. My family has been very supportive. My older sister is wonderful.[1]

"Guard your tongue from speaking evil, and your lips from deceitful speech."

—*Haffectz Hayyim, Eastern European rabbinic scholar*

☎ **United Cerebral Palsy**   **(800) 872-5827**

---

[1] **Author's note:** Wouldn't it be nice if people would say, "How wonderful that this young man has a regular job and does not expect the government to take care of him." People need to think positively about physically challenged persons who help themselves. He is going on with his life.

Part 3

PHYSICALLY
IMPAIRED

SEVERELY HANDICAPPED CHILD

Roberta is a very devoted mother of four children. The interview was very inspiring.

Our son Joseph had meningitis when he was an infant. We were told of all the multitude of things that could be wrong. You have no idea of what's wrong because at that age they are not grown enough for doctors to diagnose these things.

At five months he couldn't lift his head from my shoulder. Joseph didn't start walking, even assisted, until he was eight years old. The aftereffects of the meningitis left him blind, almost deaf and his all-around physical abilities severely impaired.

Often I would come home crying. So called well-meaning people would ask questions for which I didn't have answers. They would voice *very shallow* concern. Maybe we should be grateful they were interested.

I used to be overly sensitive to their inquisitiveness. It became overpowering. So I shy away from those kinds of persons. As Joseph grew older we all grasped for cures and solutions. At one point my grandmother was telling me what I should do with my child. For many years I had a bitter resentment against her. I distanced myself from her because I didn't want her opinion. I think a parent's intuition, the one who cares for them daily has the ultimate answers. Often we know more than doctors. We might not know the solutions, but we know the symptoms and what's going on.

My husband and I make our own decisions on what is best for him. Even now, I realize that my brothers and sisters are closer to Joseph, but if I try to bring myself closer to them we are back to the *well-meaning* clichés. I don't want to be told what to do. I have to deal with that. It's on the back burner and I won't let it surface.

Over the years people can't comprehend what goes on, what you feel, the day-to-day maintenance of a child like this. Sometimes I need a break from the daily care.

This biggie cliché, "You are doing such a good job!" You may think that I take it out of context, that they were being nice. Why is it that when a cliché is uttered the person who says it is ALWAYS excused, instead of feeling bad for the receiver? THINK! Strange is it not? They didn't know what to say? What a poor excuse. As the primary caregiver I take most of the emotional burden.

I cringe when I hear, "I don't know how you do it!" It isn't an option. You do what you have to do. Our family isn't like most families. On the spur of the moment we can't do things that other families take for granted. For example, we can't spontaneously say, "Let's go to the mall, go to the movies, or out to dinner." There are many places that we can't take Joseph. My husband and I take turns taking the other children out. Someone has to always be home with him. He isn't a burden, but he can't be left alone in the house. My mother-in-law lives close by and at times watches Joseph so we can do things as a family. She is a great help.

On occasions Joseph has gone to the mall with us. It is carefully planned. I know his moods, how he feels as I have always been around him. I know when he is hungry and wants his diaper changed, also when he is tired of sitting on the floor or being in his rocking chair. I can interpret his needs because he can't tell me, but because I know him. At the mall people will stare, kids especially, they are curious; by the same token it's hard. Often when children speak in front of mine they will say that their brother is *retarded*. Children are especially mean. Parents are responsible to educate, explain to them why some people have disabilities so in adulthood they will be more sensitive.

He is a joy to be around, he loves me unconditionally. If you ask for a kiss, he sticks out his face. He will hold you and hug you. He is pure angelic, sweet child who is spoiled rotten. He has the capabilities of about one year to eighteen months. I don't foresee any drastic improvement. We only hope for no regression and to be able to maintain his very limited abilities. It takes a daily program.

Engage Brain Before Speaking

My husband is very supportive and there is usually a 50 percent divorce rate in marriages with severely handicapped children. Joseph loves his daddy.

I have fought like cats and dogs with DES (Department of Economic Security) and we received no help, nothing. Now Joseph needs a wheelchair desperately. We were told that *maybe* they would pay for one. Due to lack of activities Joseph doesn't burn calories even though he is on a low calorie diet; I can barely lift him and walk him. Help would give years to keep him among us opposed to an institution, which would be much more expensive, and we don't want that. It's the way it is.[1]

It has been a long eight years, his life expectancy could be as long as mine. I don't have to shelter myself from the harsh outside world — the unmeaning souls who say cruel remarks. The following remark was very upsetting,

"You must be very special people for God to give you a child like Joseph."

In our congregation, Joseph is now accepted unconditionally. They let him sing in his own way. I am very

---

1   Author's note: Roberta is in a role she was totally unprepared for. Telling her and other caregivers that they are doing a *good job* is offensive. Love and TLC (Tender loving care) are not jobs. We need to remember that caregivers are under a lot of pressure. They might seem *touchy* or overly *sensitive*. At times they are. Why not? Their usual patience capacity is decreased, the reserve depleted. Could you do better?

Why can't we treat the Robertas, the unsung caregivers, gently, with love and understanding.

sensitive to the fact people will greet one of us by name but won't greet Joseph. Everyone needs to remember that despite his multitude of handicaps, Joseph IS A HUMAN BEING.

> *"Kindness in words creates confidence.*
> *Kindness in thinking creates profoundness.*
> *Kindness in giving creates love."*
>
> *—Lao-Tzu*

HEARING IMPAIRED

Tall, with jet black hair, Rose is extremely articulate, her speech enhanced by her gestures. She has overcome her difficulties with a great deal of dignity.

I lost my hearing progressively. Adjusting was very difficult. I didn't want to be deaf. My grief was overwhelming.

Seventy-eight per cent of deaf people in America lose their hearing after the age of nineteen. That statistic is very surprising.

Deafness is unique in each of us. When I first began to lose my hearing, I didn't want to learn the sign language. I finally realized that by learning, I would be able to converse better without using interpreters. As I was progressing to profound deafness I went to a speech therapist to learn how to talk and improve my lip reading skills. She warned me that people would often make the remark, "What's the matter with you, are you deaf or something?" When I am extremely tired, I don't react well to unkind words. I want to put my hands on my hips and answer, "Yeah! So what." Also when I am apprehensive, nervous, I tend to be less articulate.

A lot of us are very articulate and don't need to be told, like children, "You read lips so well" or "You have good communications skills."

I hear tone of voice through gestures, expressions, body language or a person's stance, but hearing loss is very stressful because you are always striving to understand.

People's comments are often hurtful. Before I completely lost my hearing, people would say things to me like, "Didn't you hear me?"

When I was using hearing aids and didn't answer right away, I often would be asked, "Are your batteries down?"

I was interviewed at a radio station in Florida. The announcer asked me if I used Braille. Because I couldn't hear, I couldn't see!! How ignorant. I am glad we weren't on the air as yet. The announcer would have made a fool of himself.

While waiting for a friend in front of the airport baggage claim area, I sat in my car at the curb. A security guard grabbed my arm through the open window saying,

"Are you dumb or something?"

He wanted me to move my car. Naturally I hadn't heard him.

At a meeting a woman asked me, "How did you get here?"

I answered, "By car."

The following comment was expected.

"You *shouldn't* be driving! Sirens and all that sort of thing."

It really annoyed me. What about young people and their blasting music? Why shouldn't I drive? I have a license plate which alerts law enforcement officers and emergency personnel that the driver is deaf. I also have a special identity card. Have you ever heard of a deaf person causing an accident?

Some people are reluctant to use my telephone relay, it makes me feel bad. That's the only way I can communicate by phone.

What drives most hearing impaired people up the wall is having someone suddenly stop in the middle of a stimulating conversation and tell us how well we speak. It absolutely ruins the dialogue. Many people add, "I know a lot of deaf people. They don't talk as well as you do." I think, "Gee, here we go again!" The original conversation is totally lost and I mind that.

When President Bush said, *read my lips*, it drove me crazy. Now I often chuckle at the thought of the humorous side.

I am good at lip reading but there are times when I need to ask someone to repeat what they've said. The most aggravating answer is, "Never mind, I'll tell you later." That never comes. I have to insist, "You were going to tell me...?" The answer is invariably, "It does not matter." It's over. It's hurtful, a killer.

At a workshop of mixed disabled and non-disabled people we were asked if we had a choice which disability would we prefer. I answered a wheelchair user, because people would not doubt my disability.

One day, in a restaurant with friends using sign language and two wheelchair users it was a riot. The waitress not within my visual range of vision asked me what the man in the wheelchair wanted. Laughingly, my friend answered, "She is deaf. Who are you going to talk to?"

Advocacy is a great part of my life, but I don't feel that it should be the whole purpose of my life. I am entitled to a well-balanced life, not just being an educator. It is not so much what people say, but what they do or don't do. People who don't have visible disabilities are the most misunderstood.

"Words are plentiful, but deeds are precious."

—*Lech Walesa*

☎ National Association of the Deaf (301) 587-1788
☎ TDDY   (301) 587-1789

VISUALLY IMPAIRED

Jacob is tall, good looking. He radiates self-confidence and joie de vivre. He is a successful businessman.

I don't fit the stereotype of a blind person. I don't wear dark glasses and I am not totally blind. I have light perception, I see light and dark. People will ask me, "Why do you have a dog?"

"I am blind"

"Oh! You don't look blind."

"Well, nobody ever showed me how to look blind."

In other words, who says how blind persons should look. I am a person. I look and act the way I want.

I applied for a job and was asked for references. When I mentioned a company which trains dogs for the blind the interviewer exclaimed, "How in the world did you get involved with them?"

"I am blind."

His response was, "Oh! Can you drive a car?"

"Yes, I can drive a car, but can't see where it's going."
I wanted to say, "Are you interviewing chauffeurs, truck
drivers or sales reps?"

He kept saying, "If I were blind I don't know how I
would do this job."

I have been working at this for sixteen years and I have
all the equipment that it takes to help me function.

Often when I am in a restaurant with an able-bodied
individual, the waiter will ask them, "What will he have?"

They answer, "I don't know. Why don't you ask him?"

What I hate the worst is when I am treated in a
patronizing way. I travel nationwide and customarily will
ask a skycap to assist me to the gate. Invariably the gate
agent asks the skycap, "Where is he going?"

I respond, "I don't know where he is going, but I am
going to New York."

The agent ignores me again asking the skycap, "Does
he have a ticket?"

Again I answer for myself, "I don't know if he has one,
but I have a ticket and would like to board the plane."
Finally the agent starts talking to me.

During one of my business trips I stayed at a hotel for
a week. At the restaurant I kept getting one particular
waitress. She was a middle-aged, motherly type. One day
I ordered roast beef. She talked to me as if I was seven,
"Now, honey the garnish tray is here and here is your
drink." Upon her return with my order, she patted me on
the shoulder and said, "Honey, I had the chef slice your
beef in small pieces." I nearly went through the roof. I
don't know how much of it showed, but I was very upset

and angry. I couldn't blow up in her face, so I simply said, "Thank you."

When I was ready to pay, there was no one around so I explained to her that I appreciated the service she gave me. I understood she was trying very hard to help and make me feel comfortable, but that I wasn't a child and didn't appreciate her talking as if I was and that I was capable of cutting my own meat. If, in the future, she was going to serve someone who was visually impaired or in a wheelchair all she had to do was to talk to them like her other customers. Also if she felt they needed assistance, the best thing would be to ask them and to not arbitrarily assume that they needed help. She took it very well. However, I don't know if she put my advice into practice.

At one time I used to have a full beard. I received many compliments on how good it looked. One day a woman asked me who trimmed it for me. I told her the same person who puts on my underwear for me. Often people will look at my clothes and ask, "Who dressed you this morning?" Most of the time I will say, "I don't understand your question. I am perfectly capable of putting my own clothes on." What they really want to ask is, "How did you match your clothes so well?"

People are afraid of saying the word *blind* or using the words *look, see* and *watch*. In an airport jetway the agent said, "Come down this way. You have to *watch*, OOOH! No, I shouldn't have said that."

"What?" I asked him.

"I was going to tell you to watch your step."

"You can say that word. It doesn't bother me. It is part of our vernacular and you can't change it. When I leave, I will tell you, see you later!"

I learned in my training to ask specific questions. Is the men's room to my right? Not, where is the men's room. Then the answer is vague, usually an *over there* response. Close your eyes and tell me where over there is. I need specific information.

One time before I got a dog, I was traveling by bus using a cane. I ran into a delightful young fellow in the terminal who was about twelve years old. I had heard someone playing a pinball machine so I stopped. At that time I didn't know the person's age. I asked, "Can you tell me where the water fountain is?"

"You turn around walk about ten paces and it is right in front of you."

He couldn't have given me more specific instructions. I turned around, walked the ten paces and was in front of the water fountain. I took a drink and thought, this is great, turned around and walked back to him.

"Young man, you did such a fine job, could you tell me where the men's room is?"

"Sure, come with me."

He didn't pull or tug me. I followed the sound of his shoes.

"We are coming to a step," he cautioned me. "Now quite a few steps and a railing on your right. Turn left at the top, twelve or fourteen paces to the door." With no trouble I found the door, he came in behind me. He continued his directions, "You go down here, five to six feet. It is on your right." Excellent. He then said in his delightful southern accent, "Do you know how I know how to show a blind person where things are?"

"No, I don't. How did you find out? You do a hell of a good job."

"I saw it on television."

We struck up a friendship and the young fellow sat next to me on the bus. He told me that he was going to live with his aunt because his mom used to beat up on him. He was such a wonderful little kid.

One of the most annoying things is when people play the *blind* games. They say, "Why don't you watch where you are going?" Or, "Maybe you should be driving."

At social gatherings and in my job I meet a lot of people. Someone will come up, extend their hand, and keep on shaking, holding on, expecting me to guess who it is. I usually say, "We've got to stop holding hands in public," or I will release their hand and turn away because I am not going to play that game. It is the best way of doing it. Other times they will walk up to me, put their hand on my shoulder, tap me, "Hey, guess who?"

One idiot came behind me in a crowd and pinched me on the calf. It irritated the hell out of me so much so that I developed an instant response. Whenever he would pinch me, I would automatically kick back with my leg. It's the same thing as people on the telephone asking, "Guess who?" People would rather talk to my wife instead of me.

I have a friend about my daughter's age. She drives an old car and often has mechanical problems. Old cars are my hobby. One day I was helping her to get the car running. We needed to get some parts. I didn't take my dog, just the white cane. At the parts store, the salesman saw a blind man and a young cute gal, both greasy. He didn't know which one to address. Young girls and blind men don't work on cars. When in doubt you talk to the person the most similar to you. Since two were sighted, the salesman talked to her. I answered we want these little fittings that go in there.

After he got the parts, the salesman said, "Hey, buddy who is going to put these on for you?"

"The same person who took them off, me!"

Then he asked how could I do that? I told him I had a good set of tools.

During a trip to Niagara Falls we took the Cave of the Winds tour which takes you to the base of the falls where you feel the mist. You have to wear raincoats and boots. There is a two-foot walk called the Hurricane Walk where you are within a foot of the water coming down. You can almost reach and touch it. For a blind person there is no better way of experiencing Niagara Falls.

When I wanted to take the tour I was told, "We don't allow dogs."

I was fuming. The law says that in recreation areas accessible to the public you can't discriminate against the disabled. I went to the director's office and told them that I was mature enough to know if it is safe or not for my dog and I wanted to go down. If it is unsafe, I will not do it or I am willing to sign a waiver. He answered, "When do you want to go? And do you mind if we take pictures?"

We went down. It was quite an experience. My dog shook his head to get the water off.

I am a person first, a person who happens to be blind. So if you treat people as persons first, you will always get further.

"We are here on earth to do good for others. What the others are here for, I don't know."

— W. H. Auden

☎ The Lighthouse, Inc.   (800) 334-5497

WHEELCHAIR USER

Jill is a delightful, very independent woman in her late thirties. Her laughter is contagious. Her eighteen-year-old daughter who has a learning disability lives with her.

When I was seven a woman saw me in the wheelchair. She asked my mother if I was also retarded. Upon learning that I wasn't, the woman said, "That's really too bad, because then she would not know how bad off she is."

I could tolerate the question, but not the answer. When I was young people would say, "It's so nice that you can laugh." Implying that there is a reason I shouldn't be happy. It stuck in my mind.

I was raised to be normal, as normal as anybody could be in a wheelchair. My mom made demands as if I wasn't in a wheelchair. Her friends would ask her, "Why do you make that poor child get up so early?" Why shouldn't I get up at the same time as other children do? I was always out with the other kids. Naturally, there was always a certain amount of danger.

People would say to mom, "You shouldn't let her go with other kids and make them responsible for her. You know how dangerous that is."

My mom would answer, "My daughter is responsible for her own actions, the kids are not."

When I went out with my girlfriend, she often rode on the back of my chair or sat on my lap when we went down hills. When I was ten years old, we crashed and broke my leg. At the hospital the first thing my mom heard was, "You are not going to let her go again, are you?"

I was very scared that things would change. Mom answered, "Yes, I am going to let her go again, but not today." I was fortunate to have such a mom. Her attitude helped so much.

Often I was told, "How brave of you to go into the world this way!"

When I hear them say *this way* it makes me wonder if they would prefer that I be locked away from people's eyes where no one would have to look at me. Now that I am an adult, strangers will walk up to me and say, "What's your problem?" It is somewhat intrusive, a violation of my privacy. Even if genuinely interested in someone's problem, I wouldn't walk up to a perfect stranger and ask, "How come you are bald?" When I am in a bad mood I tell them, my husband left me, the weather is bad or I don't want to answer your stupid question.

It seems that elevators inspire people...Why there? I don't know. That's where most of the irritating questions are asked.

Out of the blue someone will say, "I have a friend just like you!" Telling me they don't hold it against me. I have been asked, "How long have you been like this?" I'll answer, "All my life." They'll often say, "That is a shame. A least you are lucky that you have not known anything different." It's like saying it's too bad you didn't die when you were born, at least you wouldn't have known life in a wheelchair. If I know someone well, and they have questions, I don't mind answering them.

Since I have been divorced, I have had an attendant help me get ready for work. When one quits, I place an ad in the paper. When people answer, first they assume that you are talking for someone else.

"What's wrong with her?"

"It's me. I am confined to a wheelchair. Let me tell you about myself."

"Oh, It's you! You don't sound like a handicapped person."

How am I supposed to sound?

"The hours are 5:30am to 7:30am, two hours, Monday through Friday."

Half the time I will get an argument from the caller, "Why does it have to be so early?"

"Because I have to be at work at 8:00am. It takes two hours to get me ready."

The next thing you can count on them saying is, "You what? *You* work?"

Nobody would laugh at me if I was at bottom of a staircase and asked for help. They wouldn't say, "You are an idiot. Why don't you walk up the stairs." Because you can't see something, does not mean it's not REAL.

When I go out with my daughter people will assume that I am retarded and will ask her questions which should be addressed to me. Jane has a learning disability. She might not know the exact change she needs in a store or be able to read a menu.

Why do people have to look down on a person who for example asks a waitress, "Can you help me with the menu? I can't read."

Jane would rather not eat than ask. I think it's terrible, people causing her embarrassment like that.

When Jane goes to special ed (education), adults say she is a *retard*. It is very damaging. Nothing could be worse for her self-esteem. The implication is a that a person should be ashamed of their disability, that there is something wrong with you as a person. If Jane hears it often enough, she will believe it. She finally dropped out of school. I am helping her to develop some independence. But I don't do things for her that she can do for herself.

We make so many judgements based on appearance, what we see, experiences we have had and often we don't have a clue. People are condescending because they walk and I can't. It took me a long time to understand how uncomfortable and guilty we make able-bodied people feel. People have been intrusive, insensitive, and have invaded my privacy.

"It's terribly easy to shake a man's faith in himself... To break a man's spirit is devil's work."

—*Candida, G. B. Shaw*

Part 4

GRIEF

CAR DEATH:
ACCIDENT

E*laine has reddish hair, eyes blazing with energy.*

In 1995, my husband Carl and our son decided to go hunting before Mike left for college. They had wanted for a long time to hunt in Wyoming near some friends' ranch. Carl had bought Mike a new car. The hunting trip was going to be a good time to test drive it.

They left on a Sunday, bright and early. Driving away Carl, smiling, blew me a kiss from the passenger seat, then both waved. Carl was supposed to call me every evening around 6pm. The following day while preparing a late dinner, our daughter Paula and I were waiting for that phone call. I still picture his smiling face. Seven o'clock had already passed then eight. Nothing! I thought that they might have wanted to drive some extra miles. At 9:30pm the phone finally rang. I left the kitchen drying my hands, walking towards the phone in the hall which had a chair next to it. In the meantime, Paula had picked up the upstairs extension. It was Mike's voice, that was odd I thought. Carl was the one who always called because he used our telephone credit card. Hearing Mike's voice I asked, "Why are you doing the calling? Where is Dad?"

"There was an accident," he hesitantly answered.

"Where is Dad?" I asked a second time putting emphasis on the word Dad.

After a long pause and with a catch in his voice Mike said, "Mom, Dad didn't make it!"

"Didn't make what, Mike? What are you talking about? Let me talk to your Dad *right now.*"

"No, Mom. He... didn't... make... it."

I kept saying over and over again, "What do you mean?" Paula ran down the stairs. Dropping the phone, I started screaming. There was no way I could understand *dead.*

Like a movie, I saw again and again Carl's smile, his kiss, waving goodbye — I didn't know for the last time. Our plans had been that by the end of the week I was to pick him up at the airport on an early flight from Cheyenne and we would have had the whole day to ourselves.

Next thing I knew I was trying to get up and fell, although I didn't remember falling. I was trying to stand. *It's not true* kept ringing in my head. When I got on the phone again, Paula was talking to Mike. He had been X-rayed, no broken bones. He was okay.

I decided to catch the first flight to Cheyenne. I needed to be there with Mike and make the necessary arrangements to bring my husband home. Paula and I feverishly

looked in telephone books for necessary numbers. Paula kept repeating, "Dad is dead, Dad is dead."

Paula and I couldn't help each other. I called all the people I could think of, friends, family, all numbers seemed busy. Finally I was able to reach a new neighbor. The husband answered, stating that his wife was at a PTA meeting. I had only met him once. I could not share the horrible news with a stranger. I called my neighbor across the street. She also was not home, but I finally was able to whisper to her husband Joe,

"Carl is dead."

There was only a gasp at the other end, then silence. In no time at all he was at the front door with two women I didn't know from the neighborhood. They started making phone calls for me. After that I didn't have any control. I can vaguely remember Joe asking me, "Where are your parents? Do you have brothers and sisters?"

In a fog, I could hear him say on the phone, "This is Joe, Norma and Carl's neighbor. I have some very bad news."

The following day, a cousin sitting in the living room said, "It's bad now, but you don't have *any* idea how bad it is going to get! It is going to be so bad for *five* years."

I kept saying to myself this cannot go on for *five* years! I cannot survive *five years*! So many people around me asking so many questions: "Have you done this, have you done that?" I was only one person. Telling me what to do or all saying the same thing. People would be there for five minutes then gone. I could not get any rest. I became angry, had the right to be angry at Carl's death, all the questions. I'll never, never be over it.

Engage Brain Before Speaking

Paula and I went twice to the funeral parlor. At one point she whispered in my ear, "Mom, they are trying to sell you everything." I didn't know until years later that I paid double the price for the funeral I should have paid.

Now in my work as a counselor, I try to help people, to let them know that during difficult times they need help. The bereaved don't reason objectively. It's hard to make sense of what has happened, too much on one's mind. At that point we are very vulnerable. The whole thing kept me very angry for a long time.

Carl had been a foreman for a large manufacturing company. He was always highly appreciated by management for his ingenuity in saving money for the company. One of his suggestions had saved more than $100,000 in operating cost. Employees were supposed to receive a percentage of all implemented suggestions. Carl hadn't received the bonus check as yet.

Several days after the funeral, the chief of personnel, Mark Schultz, called stating that I needed to sign papers regarding Carl's life insurance. When I got to his office, the amount was a lot less than Carl had told me it should be. I didn't have a copy of the policy. Before I left, Mark mentioned that a check would be mailed for the bonus. On the way out I passed by my husband's little office, the chair he should have been sitting on behind his desk. I sobbed all the way to the car.

A week after the funeral, an acquaintance told me, and later wrote a note, "Please call if I can help."

I called her, and she said, "Why don't you come over?"

I agreed to go after I took a cold shower to calm myself down. When I got there she started telling me all of her

68

problems, talked for two hours. She finally told me that I would not know what pain was until after a year and half. Leaving, I thought, I think that I am going out of my mind. Is that what people call compassion? They basically want to help themselves, hear their own sadness.

Her husband had also been killed in an auto accident, but the accidents were not similar. Carl's accident was caused by negligence. A cow that should have been penned up by a farmer had strayed. Carl was coming around a bend of the road over a small hill with limited visibility. He hit the cow head on.

A few weeks after the funeral I called personnel to inquire about Carl's bonus. Mark Schultz said it would be paid. I waited a month, nothing. I called again asking for Mark. I was advised that he had resigned. The bonus could not be paid. I asked why? The company had nothing in writing. I received nothing. I was absolutely crushed, but I was powerless. I didn't know how to go from having money to not having any.

Many ignorant people are no longer my friends. Shortly after Carl's death, my other daughter Anna got very sick. I had to take her to the hospital. No one could find out what was wrong with her. People started to tell me, "You *have to* quit worrying so much. You *have to* calm down. You *have to* learn how to deal with this stress." I got sick of *HAVE TOs*.

When Paula was ready to leave to return to college I was again told, "You shouldn't worry about her." Why shouldn't I? I was always concerned about my children when they were gone. Since Carl's death, I worry even more. It was easy for people to spout those empty words, clichés. They went on with their lives.

A woman that I had known a long time called, telling me she was going to a stress reduction group, why didn't I join her? I wanted to scream, "Leave me alone."

Three months after the funeral I received a call from the plant where my eldest son Mike had a summer job. He had been badly hurt. He was in the emergency room. I again collapsed screaming, " I've heard it all. I've heard it all."

When I arrived at the hospital, he had been admitted. Mike had been crushed between some crates that had not been secured. He was in intensive care. If you think the stress was bad before! But as Mike healed, people still told me I needed to calm down.

If my husband Carl had been alive we could have shared our pain. We could have comforted each other. Tell him when I was not feeling well emotionally and physically. Now I am alone because of someone's negligence.

Basically people are not stupid. They don't *think*. They just can't connect or relate.

I was so down that I decided to see a grief counselor. Kay had a gentle and prissy voice. First thing she asked was, "Is it hard to accept your husband's death?" After two months? Was she *nuts*? After all, I was seeing her because it was hard. She did most of the talking, telling me what to do instead of letting me talk. Could not tell her my needs. At that time I lived angry.

"Think positive and keep busy," she repeated, advice I'd already heard a hundred times.

After that remark I told her all the things I had to do alone since my husband's death. "Is that busy enough for you," I sarcastically asked her. No encouragement. She thought that because I had severe traumas, I should do everything she told me without explanation. She made me feel more vulnerable and controlled. I needed empowerment.

Another time she again asked, "Can't you accept your husband's death?"

I finally got mad at her, got hysterical. "He is dead on account of a cow, someone's negligence. I enjoyed seeing him in the casket, the dirt thrown over him."

I don't like the word *closure*. Does it mean that I have to forget Carl? I am still very angry now, but to a lesser degree. Acceptance does not mean closure. Finally I got sick of Kay telling me not to let my church tell me what to think. I was emotionally broken. I told her off, never went back.

When I see my grandchild I can't keep from thinking that Carl will never see him. The anger comes back. Who can I tell? New things will bring new feelings about him. So many times I want to share things with him.

After I moved to this state, I took a real estate course. As soon as I got my license I was immediately asked, "Are you making any sales, making money?"

Why should they worry if I do or not? Because I hold two jobs I am constantly told, "You do too much, you should slow down. You are going to get sick." It seems strange to me that people love to tell others what to do. So what if I go overboard? It's *my* life.

I had good advice from a nun, "Don't rely on medication for your grief. It's a process that one needs to go through."[1]

"You can't prevent birds of sorrow from flying over your head but, you can prevent them from building nests in your hair."

—*Chinese proverb*

☎ **AARP Widowed Persons Service** (202) 434-2260

---

[1] **Author's note:** Grief support groups are very helpful. One can vent one's anger without judgement. Everyone needs acceptance.

CHILD'S DROWNING

Nina, *a telephone company representative, lives in Florida with her husband and three children.*

Our two-year-old child drowned a year ago, at a friend's house. I had left Rob at Marie's so I could keep a dental appointment. She has a fenced pool and an area next to it where her children play.

Marie went in the house to get clean clothes because Rob had spilled a drink all over himself. She changed him, went back into the house to put his dirty clothes with a load of wash. When she returned he was face down in the pool.

At the hospital it really bothered me when a nurse put a tape recorder near him playing lullabies thinking it would comfort him. He was in a coma and I didn't think he could hear. The music really disturbed me. We knew that he was never going to wake up. It was intended as a comforting gesture, but it seemed too clinical and hurt so bad. I would never sing lullabies to him and never see him go to sleep.

Afterwards people said, *"AT LEAST* HE DIDN'T SUFFER!"* It was very disturbing. How in the world would they know? The drowning might not have lasted that long, but he must have been frightened. It was still bad.

What is suffering?

Does it take an extended length of time to count suffering? His death had to be terrifying.

Another hurtful cliché that many people said, "At least you had him for two years." Even though they were trying to comfort me I wanted to scream at them, "How can you say that? What is time? My baby is dead." Grief is grief. I have some friends who lost children when they miscarried or at birth. Their grief is just as real.

I have gone back to work and am trying to lead a normal life. People say, "I don't know how you can do it!" The way I look at it, I don't have a choice. I have to do it. My choice would be to have my son back. We need to continue living as a wounded family. They don't know what else to say. People who make those remarks are neither helpful or supportive. Better say *nothing*.

There was a lot of finger pointing by the media. They used the word *constant* supervision as a guideline to go by, but in everyday living with a two-year old you can't watch them every second. People didn't say it to me, but I heard nasty comments second hand about Marie. She should have done this, done that. The message from the media was, "You need to watch them. You need a fence." All these are true, but all those precautions were taken. The accident still happened. Marie was hysterical and was treated on the scene. I am sure she has been torturing herself ever since. I don't blame Marie for what happened.

My husband remembers things that were not said. It is very therapeutic for us and anyone who had gone through a child's drowning to talk about it. My husband's male friends change the subject whenever he talks about our son, Rob. They don't know what to say and that hurts more. He doesn't have a close friend with whom he can talk. He gets very depressed, withdrawn and won't talk about it with me.

I explained to my supervisor that some days a little thing will trigger memories like a customer with the same name as my son's. Part of my job is to interview people applying for new telephone service. I need to ask them their occupation and during a particular interview a man told me that he worked for a pool company. I was so shaken that it took me fifteen minutes to stop trembling.

I saw a woman interviewed on TV who also had a little girl drown in a pool. Someone from the audience asked her, "How can you be so calm talking about this tragic death?" It is very helpful to continue talking about it and mention the circumstances. The more you talk about it, the easier it is to accept it ourselves. It's very true. Please, let us talk about the loss of our child.

> "The grief that does not speak whispers
> The o'erfaugth heart and bids it break."
>
> —*Shakespeare*

☎ Compassionate Friends National Office
(for parents who have lost a child) (708) 990-0010

DRUNK DRIVER/ SUICIDE

Sibyl is a very articulate woman. She lives with her husband in a beautifully decorated townhouse. She is an interior decorator and her husband owns a barber shop.

I lost my twenty-one-year-old son to suicide. Of course it is the S word you have deal with. The worst is the instant shock. After the funeral I took my daughter Louise to the doctor's. He had heard about Bob's suicide. I told him how upset I was. He said, "Maybe, it was for the best!" What a terrible thing to say to me. Still in shock, I didn't even respond. Later I was thinking, for the *best*! Would that doctor say that if it had happened to his son? Where did that come from? It's for the *best*! I don't know why but every now and then it pops into my mind and I feel like going to his office and asking him, "What did you mean, it was for the *best*?" It was nine years ago and the words are still bugging me. It does not dawn on you what someone said to you until later.

Some people tell me, "I don't know what to say. I want to give you a hug. I want you to know that I am thinking about you." That's very helpful.

Most people think that when a person commits suicide, they are mentally ill. One question frequently asked to parents, "Were they always crazy?" There is the social stigma, shame and rejection attached to suicide.

When it comes to suicide, people sometimes say very hurtful comments which they would not say under other circumstances.

Time heals all wounds...people think that if one ignores grief, it will go away. It doesn't, you need to work through it. If you don't work through it, it will wait for you. Four years after our Bob's death, our only daughter Louise was killed by a drunk driver as she was coming home from baby sitting. His car smashed into hers, and her car exploded. The fact that she burned was even harder to accept. Her birthday is coming up real soon, I am getting knots in my stomach. This second loss made it even more difficult for people. I actually felt sorry for our friends having to deal with us. How could they know what to do or say.

Last month was my son Bob's death anniversary. In the fall I wasn't sure if I was up to attending an out-of-town conference for family members of suicide victims. I was going with a couple of people from my state whose child died under similar circumstances. They assured me they would look after me because my brain was not working very well at that time. The keynote speech was delivered by an author who had lost a child to suicide. During his lecture he stated that it is estimated that in the US daily, eighty-three people commit suicide — sixty percent with firearms.

After the talk, I lined up with other people to speak to him. I told him about Bob and Louise's deaths. Smiling he looked at me saying, "Well, now you have the tools to deal with this latest death!" He was telling me, you have done this before, this is going to be a breeze! I was dumbfounded. What? A breeze? I know this man goes around helping people. I don't think he really thought that through. I knew from reading his books that he has three or four other children. Would he feel that way if he lost another child? For my husband and I, Louise and Bob were all we had. That you need to gather your tools to deal with losses is true and very good. But, somehow I didn't appreciate him stating that I had the tools thus I was okay. It was the equivalent of saying, you should know how to deal with the death of your daughter, no problem. It shows that we *all* say hurtful words, things that we regret. But from HIM?

A week after a woman's husband committed suicide she was told, "You know, you should not be wearing your wedding ring. Really, you are no longer married to him." After all she can wear it as long as she wants, it's her business.

Because it was told by a friend, it hurt her even more badly. Spouses get a lot of clichés thrown at them, "When are you going to start dating. Put it behind you."

A couple I met at a support group related this incident. They were told by a therapist that they were not doing the right thing by planting a tree in their daughter's memory. It was glamorizing suicide. But the tree was in memory of her life not how it ended. What would the therapist say about the rose garden for my daughter and the bird feeder for my son who loved birds? How could he say such a thing? How out of touch with reality that therapist was. But the husband had a good answer. "We have war memorials. It does not mean we like wars. We are not going to forget those men. Why should we forget our children?" It is things like that are important to us.

Questions which are commonly asked, "Do you know why? Were there any signs? Didn't you pay attention to the clues?" For many parents there aren't any clues. Those questions make the loss very hard. With our son Bob's suicide, it came out of the blue. It seems to happen that way with young people. Parents think everything is going all right.

I knew a young boy of fifteen. One day, at school during the lunch break he told a friend that he was going home to pick up something he had forgotten. He never came back. His younger sister found him in his bedroom, dead, a gun on the floor. To this day his parents don't know the reason why. What was wrong? What happened?

It seems that more boys commit suicide than girls, but with girls there are more attempts, usually with overdose. Among older people there's a new phenomenon, the homicide/suicide. One of them is seriously sick and at their age can't fathom living alone. They decide to go together. It is very hard on the children.

Dealing with the courts was horrendous. The worse was to find out that the man who killed my daughter was going to serve only half of his time. I was fit to be tied. The justice system has it's own agenda, that's the way it goes. The judge asked, "Do you want him to serve seven and half years?" But that's not the way it is—they are released on work furlough. The reason they are given work furlough at this point is to give them a chance so they can prove themselves before they are coming up for parole.

Later we received a letter that he was coming up for parole. He has already got the best deal. We didn't understand so I called to find out, "What do you mean by that?" I was given the understanding that he was going to be home by this time. Try to be a good boy in order to see if he could get paroled. Finally my husband and I had to decide to *let it go*, hoping that the system knew what it was doing and that this guy would not be a repeat offender and hurt other families the way we've been hurt. Getting on with our daily life takes all our energy.

Recently I went to a health fair. While I was looking at material on MADD (Mothers Against Drunk Drivers) I heard a woman ask the man behind the display table, "Are you involved with this because you lost someone to a drunk driver?"

"Yes," was the answer.

The woman added, "You know if people die without becoming born again Christians they will go to hell." Can you *imagine*! How gross! How unthinkable all in the name of religion. I am sure God doesn't like these kind of Christians. Why would she take that approach. One would think that she would be more interested in what actions should be taken against drunken drivers. But our society is programmed to blame victims thus diverting our attention from the perpetrators. She probably only wanted everyone to know that she was a born again Christian.

I can't deal with, "It's God's will." Everyone has their own beliefs, some believe that God decides everything that happens. I couldn't live with that, if I thought God decided that my kids should die the way they did. I would be angry with him. God is there to help us go through our suffering. I believe he never decided that Louise on her way home was going to be killed by a drunk driver. I have been told many times, "You must forgive." I am not that big of a person.[1]

I soon found out that in grief memory gets really bad. "I am going crazy, can't remember anything!" Someone asked me, "How long does it take to go away?" The answer was, "We are still waiting."

People don't understand that we *need* to talk of the family members who died. Few people, when you bring up your losses know it's okay to talk about them. Others don't. We want to keep them with us. We don't want to forget them, wipe them out of our lives. One does not erase loved ones. Some people's families hurry up and change the subject when the talk reverts to the departed. That's why support groups are so important.

---

[1] **Author's note:** "God forgives. Me, I am only human." (heard on TV)

A long time friend, Janet knew my children well. We really enjoy reminiscing. Both of my kids were real characters. She will think of something that reminds her of them, and call me, "Do you remember this incident...?" Bless her heart, she actually has notes, cards and letters written back and forth between her children and mine. She has a letter from my then nine-year-old to her son. At that time Louise was six. I treasure those things.

Holidays, birthdays and anniversaries are bad. I spend that time with my kids, and I don't want anyone bothering me. I look at my albums. For my daughter's birthday I go to my beautiful rose garden. I need something physical, like working in the garden. It helps me to work through all this. I have a feeling of peacefulness.

Some people think that you are better off going on about your business. That we don't want to be reminded, don't want to be called. I have a very special friend who calls regularly, "I wanted to let you know that I was thinking about you. Do you want to talk or would you rather not? Do you want to go out to lunch?" Her friendship is very precious to me.

I always tell people, "Don't let anyone tell you *how* to grieve." Whatever helps you is the right way to do it, not what someone else tells you. One of the main complaints I have is when people tell me, "You have to get on with your life! It's been a whole year."

The first year I felt absolutely nothing, I didn't even know I was here. Some people feel that the second year gets worse instead of better. There is a line in a movie that always stuck in my mind, it's so true. It was about a father whose son was at the wrong place and wrong time during a hold up. He was shot. The father/actor said, "The first year it was like a bad dream. The second is for *real*."

All the shock is worn off, one is really dealing with the grief, the loss. The loneliness, the longing that you have, that is worse. I don't like that they are further away from me. During that first year you can say, "Last year this time we were doing this, remember that." After that year those memories are taken away from you. Last year is dead. You don't have that, and it's very painful. You think of how long it's been since you held them, kissed them, talked to them.

"Things can't get any worse." I don't say that anymore.

The night before my son's girlfriend Jane shot herself I told him the same cliché. He was naturally extremely upset. You need to help her get through this. She'd been raped. The following day she was dead... It got worse. How could I have said that?

When Jane was raped, she called my son. My husband and son met her at the hospital and brought her back here to our house in the suburbs. We didn't want her to go back to her apartment alone until she found another one. She insisted on sleeping one more night at her place before she moved. We tried to discourage her, but to no avail. Jane wanted also to finish packing.

That night she went to work at the hospital working the night shift. During a break Jane told her supervisor that no one was ever going to get to her again. She showed her a gun in her purse. Her supervisor thought that she meant that if anyone tried messing with her again, they were going to get shot. The following day Bob called Jane several times. Not receiving an answer he drove to her place.

He was shocked to find the door unlocked. He found her on her bed, still in her nurse's uniform. She had shot herself. Bob was devastated, refused to talk about it.

I feel God understands people's limits especially when it involves human cruelty. How can one be angry with oneself? I can't deal with that stuff anymore. One of my son's friends recently tried to commit suicide. He is on a breathing machine. How much pain does his father want him to take? His dad is going to have a hard time dealing with it. When you are at the point that you are not yourself anymore, can't function, why allow the suffering?

Suicide is something I thought I would never have to deal with. My husband and I *now* have no children. We are alone. We often think that when we are older and sick we might consider suicide.

"To say that everything works in God's world may be comforting to the casual bystander, but it is an insult to the bereaved and the unfortunate."

—*Rabbi Harold S. Kushner*

☎ MADD (Mothers Against Drunk Drivers)
(214) 744-6233; (800) 438-6233

WIDOW

White-haired Florence has dark eyes that show a lot of sadness. Her husband of forty-seven years died after of long battle with cancer.

A month after the funeral, Florence received a devastating letter from her oldest daughter, Nancy who lived in an eastern state. She shared its contents with me. After the usual family news, Nancy listed cliché after cliché, empty words robbing her mother of her grief.

"You are better off than others. Here are a few of the ways you are luckier than other widows. You should be grateful that he is not suffering anymore. You wouldn't want him lingering so you would have him longer."

How hurtful! Naturally her mom was the last one to want her husband to suffer. Florence is grieving for herself, her loss, and the emptiness.

Nancy doesn't know what it feels like to wake up in the middle of the night, an empty space in the bed. To no longer hear a car door slamming in the garage, his booming voice from the door, "Hi! Hon. I am home." A voice she will never hear again.

"You have a beautiful home."

It does not ease the pain of seeing his empty favorite chair, no longer smelling the aroma of his pipe. The empty spot across the dinner table.

"You have your health! You have good health coverage. Think of all the uninsured."

Will Nancy come and take care of her Mom if she gets sick?

In the letter Nancy listed the names of relatives who were in poor health. Empty words, empty words.

"Your children are healthy and independent."

They were before their father died.

"You had forty-seven good years with Dad!"

Yes, a long time. Grief is not measured by years. Grief is grief.

"You have a car and you know how to drive."

Yes, her husband's car. Florence is of another generation. She stayed home to take care of her seven children. Her husband did most of the driving, now she doesn't feel too comfortable driving in traffic.

"You are loved by your children and grandchildren."

Yes, but it can't replace her husband's love.

"Force yourself to go out."

Florence might do that later, in the meantime she needs to grieve. The last thing she needs right now is a litany of empty words and directives. Her grief needs to be acknowledged.

The very phrase *grief process* tells it all. Bland, neutral, words that have nothing to do with an individual's personal loss. It sounds like a recipe. Grief is a very personal journey.[1]

Our society gives the message that losses should be resolved quickly. Typical clichés to the widowed:

It's been two years! Are you still grieving? You should be over the loss by now.
Get on with your life, stop moping.
Why don't you want to get married again? You must have had a bad marriage.

"My religion is very simple. My religion is kindness."

—The Dalai Lama

☎ **AARP Widowed Persons Service   (202) 434-2260**

---

1   **Author's note:** We are a throw away society. Something breaks — throw it away and replace it.

A widow was told, "Don't worry, God will give you another husband!" Since when does God hand out husbands?

WIDOWER

Donald is short with abundant wavy salt and pepper hair. He is a retired sheriff from a small Midwest town. He has an infectious laugh. His wife of forty years died of kidney cancer.

Since my wife Dorothy's death a year ago I have found myself at loose ends. On my street live several families: a widow Ida across the street with two teenage children; next door a middle-aged couple, Robert and Rachel. His business takes him away, often a couple of weeks at a time. Before my wife's death we visited each other, played cards. Often using the back doors of our houses, walking in after knocking. My wife and Rachel were good friends, visiting each other over a cup of coffee.

Since Dorothy's death occasionally Rachel has asked me to make little repairs that could not wait until her husband's return. I do the same for Ida. Rachel has also asked me to share her dinner. Why not? We both talk about our spouses as we miss them. I have taken her out to dinner. When Robert calls from overseas he always asks Rachel, "Are you taking care of Donald?" When he is back in town he is always concerned about my well-being.

I try to do things for neighbors. First, it keeps me busy and second, it makes me feel good. Another neighbor, Ralph called me one day to pick him up at work as his carpool partner had gone home sick. I asked Rachel to go with me for company. We arrived downtown too early so I asked Rachel to go in the building, and call Ralph. When Ralph answered the phone he said, "What are you doing on the phone? *Where* is Donald?" Like Rachel was not supposed to be there.

Our society can't accept people the way they are without reading something that is not there. Why can't we accept *friendship* between men and women. So the closest neighbors check up on my friendship with Rachel.

One funny incident. One morning I went to Rachel's for coffee. I wasn't there longer than ten minutes before who was at the back door knocking but Ida! Later she told me, "You are seeing a lot of Rachel." Well, after all we are free and way over twenty-one. Even my son has made remarks about Rachel and me.

I believe in being kind and helping others regardless of their sex.

Someone asked me the craziest of questions. "Are you going to move?" What a question? Because I lost a wife, I have to go somewhere else! Another person said, "God wanted her back with him!"

"The center of human nature is rooted in ten thousand ordinary acts of kindness that define our days."

—*Stephen Jay Gould*

☎ AARP Widowed Persons Service   (202) 434-2260

MISCARRIAGE

S*hattered hopes.*

How devastating to carry a new life which ends before term.

How insensitive to tell a woman grieving for the little one who will never live.

"Just about every woman miscarries. You are young, it's nothing. Next time it will work."

How can someone make light of it? Instantaneously it is birth and death. Shattered hopes.

"It was meant to be. You are better off, probably a bad sperm. Something would have been wrong with the baby. It's nature's way of discarding the imperfect."

How awful to tell a woman that the baby she carried in her womb was better off not going full term. Where in the world do people get that sickening supposed wisdom?

"God wanted little angels in heaven." What a cruel God! Robbing women for His pleasure! If only people would listen to themselves talk!

Engage Brain Before Speaking

"God plucks the best flowers for his garden!" Listen carefully! Think those words through. Sounds like a God who kills unborn babies! Like humans cut flowers to decorate a room. Absolutely *insane*.

Comment to a childless woman, "You are better off and lucky not to have children." How vicious when a woman has wanted children so much. No child will ever call her Mom. "At least you didn't have to listen to them cry during the night." As if not acknowledging the joys of parenting makes longing for children foolish. Very comforting.

A woman confided that she'd had two miscarriages. During her third pregnancy her doctor suggested that she and her husband refrain from intercourse. One day her husband forced himself on her. Colleen miscarried twin girls at five and half months. They lived a couple of hours. She received no moral support from her husband. She received no moral support from her husband. When she was well enough, Colleen went back to work; that's it. Nobody talked about her loss. No support.

Colleen is constantly reminded of her lack of children. When women of her generation get together often the topic of conversation is children and grandchildren. She can't participate. When she doesn't take part Colleen is asked, "Don't you have children?" "No." As if it was a sin. Women in general are not kind toward childless women.

The most commonly used cliché to childless women, often said in a very casual way,

"You can always *adopt*."

Mother's day is a yearly reminder.

Miscarriages are invisible losses. The mother doesn't see those little ones who will never be. Colleen's loss of her twins was hers, hers to grieve.

Good thing to say, "I am so sorry you had that loss. I hope you feel better soon."

You are acknowledging the loss. That alone helps, you are not making light of it.

Hugs are wonderful! A touch of a hand helps healing of broken hearts. Human contact.

In his book "Blood Sport" James B. Stewart states, "You can't be a woman if you don't have children. It's the central mission of women!" Fortunately, women themselves have challenged this pernicious social cliché.

Am I an *it*?

"L'enfer, c'est les autres." (*Hell is others*)

—*Jean-Paul Sartre*

☎ Compassionate Friends National Office
(For parents who have lost a child)   (708) 990-0010

STILLBIRTH

Marge is in her late thirties, very athletic and vivacious. She lives with her husband and children in a charming cottage overlooking the Pacific Ocean.

I got pregnant one year after we were married. My pregnancy progressed fine, no complications except some morning sickness. My due date was April 30. I took a maternity leave starting the day I was due. May 2, my husband had gone to work in San Francisco. We lived about thirty-five miles away. I had a back-up driver, my friend Ruth. After I got up that morning, my water broke. I called Ruth, she wasn't there. I had to call David because I didn't know many of my neighbors. We had moved six months previously from the east coast. I called my doctor. His nurse asked me if I had any contractions. No, I wasn't in active labor. The nurse advised me to come to the office before I went to the hospital because it was only a block away. While waiting for David I called my mother.

In the doctor's office while the nurse was examining
me, more fluid came out.

She didn't think anything of it. By then it was eleven
in the morning. She asked me to be at the hospital by two
in the afternoon.

My husband and I made a decision to go to the hospital
right away. I was prepared, put in a hospital gown. The
nurse checked me, she couldn't find the baby's heartbeat.
The doctor came, he said that sometimes it can't be found
because of the way the baby is positioned. So he put in
an internal monitor. The baby had died.

We didn't know at that time what had caused the death.
It could only be speculated that when I had lost that gush
of water the baby came down and that's when it happened.
A decision needed to be made. How was I to deliver? My
doctor discouraged me from having a C (caesarian) section. It can complicate subsequent deliveries. Why do one
if it is not necessary?

Here I was laying with a dead child inside of me! I was
numb. The doctor proceeded to induce active labor. That
evening I delivered. He saw the umbilical cord first and
knew right away the cause of death. When I lost the water
in the doctor's office the cord had dropped between my
pelvic bone and the baby's head cutting the oxygen off.
The baby, was eight pounds ten ounces, a baby boy,
twenty-five inches long. We named him Gary after his
maternal grandfather. My baby was a perfect little boy.
An autopsy was performed, nothing was wrong.

It was a very trying time for my husband and I. It was
our first child, and we'd looked forward so much to the
birth. To find out that I was going to deliver a dead baby

was very traumatic. After the birth I didn't want to see my baby. My doctor sent a social worker to talk to me.

She said, "Marge you really need to see your son. You may feel now that you don't, but a few years down the road you might be standing at the sink peeling potatoes and go berserk wishing you had seen your son. I know it is real hard for you right now."

So we made provisions to bring the baby into the room and have me hold him. I couldn't get myself to do that. Or I could go down to the morgue where they would have him laying on a table behind a curtain. That's the decision we made. We went down with our pastor and the social worker. We did get to view him, but I didn't hold him.

To this day I feel that I made the right decision. Maybe somebody else would have made another decision, they might have wanted to hold the baby. I couldn't bear at that time to hold him in my arms.[1]

After that we had another decision to make. What do we want to do as far as funeral arrangements? Naturally we were caught off guard. We were not prepared for any of this. It was the furthest thing from our minds. We had been ready to celebrate the birth of our child, but not the death of our son.

Due to my husband's military career we moved a lot, so we didn't have any roots anywhere, no cemetery plot. Our families offered burial in our home state of Oregon.

---

[1] **Author's Note:** We are all unique. We all need to make decisions appropriate to our needs. It is a time when people need not be showered with *shoulds*.

We discussed it, talked to the nurse and the social worker. We asked about what most people do in situations like ours. We were told that many didn't want to go through a funeral, we had the hospital take care of the cremation. It didn't matter where Gary was buried, he was in heaven. One day when we have a plot we will have a headstone made.

It was a very trying time for us. If it had not been for our religion we would have had a rougher time. We had no family around us. Five days later my mother came, after allowing us to grieve on our own. It was real hard, our church was our family.

We had a small memorial service one evening at the church with only the pastor, my husband and I. We wrote a prayer which we read out loud. Gary would be twelve this year.

It doesn't matter how old a child is, there is a special bonding. He was a part of me for nine months. He is not with me, but he is still a part of me. He was not taken away from me completely even though God has his soul.

After our son's death, people called, some sympathetic but others saying hurtful clichés:

The reason why your son is not with you, God knows.
There is a reason for all this.
God had another purpose for Gary to serve than being with you.
I think God had a plan.

I know they try to comfort you. But speaking for God! I felt, Why me? A brief life is not an incomplete one. I was also told, "I don't know what to say." It was the best anyone could tell me. It didn't hurt!

Engage Brain Before Speaking

The most comforting was when people told us, "We are here for you if you need us," and meant it.

A very hard thing to do was taking the nursery down. People offered to help, but we knew that my husband and I needed to do it alone. When my mother came she slept were the nursery was.

The worst occurred when I went back to work. I worked as a secretary in a large utility company office. A lot of the employees knew me by sight, at the copying machine, or walking around. They knew that I'd been pregnant.

The girls would come over, "Oh! you had your baby!" I had to explain to everybody, I shouldn't have had to. It was extremely hard. I would say, "I had a child, but my son was stillborn."

Some would say, "I am so sorry." Many didn't stop there. They would add, "You are still young, you can have more. I am *sure* you could have more." How in the world could they know? You are still young kept on popping out. I knew I might have more but I still grieved Gary's death. So many people are insensitive.

No one realizes what *hell* I went through to have my next two. I went through infertility treatments to have my daughter and son who are now nine and five. We spent thousands of dollars.

When people ask me how many children I have, Gary's birth is always acknowledged. I wear his birthstone on my mother's ring, even though I didn't spend any time with him.

I am grateful that someone didn't come and say, "Did you do something bad? Were you a bad person. Did you do something you are paying the price for?"

It was very hard for me to go to department stores, walk down the baby clothes aisle. Hard to see other pregnant women.

I liked the way some people responded by sending us poems, articles because they could not express verbally how they felt.

Sometimes my husband would say, "I'll never see Gary grow up. I'll never be able to take him to a baseball game." Sure we have our other children, we enjoy them but they won't have their older brother.

At work I didn't realize that another woman was pregnant, due two months after me. She lost her child at the seventh month. I felt that I was blessed to be able to share with her some of the feelings that I went through. I didn't really know the woman until we both got pregnant. She would come to my office and we would chit chat. Before she came back to work I wrote her a long letter telling her she could call or see me at any time. When I later saw her at the office she thanked me and told me how she appreciated my caring and sharing.

Shortly after I returned to work a co-worker, a close friend got pregnant. She felt so bad. She thought, "Why did I get pregnant? This timing is not perfect." I told her not to feel that way. "Be happy. I am for you. One day I will be pregnant too."

Six months later my husband was transferred to Dallas. In a way it was good, we were moving out of the house because every time I walked into the former nursery, memories would drown me.

Where we moved all our neighbors had children. The women would visit, sit around talking about their children. It was real hard. I couldn't partake in the conversations. But three months later I found out that I was pregnant. The baby was born with the cord around his neck. He was blue, but started screaming and has not stopped ever since!

My children know about their brother Gary. Sometimes they say that they wish he was alive so they could have another playmate. Mother's Day and his birthday are hard on me. My husband gives me extra hugs. Last Mother's Day, in church singing, I choked up and started crying. I can't say that it has gotten any easier. I try to visualize what Gary would have looked like now. I don't have any concrete place to pay my respects. No headstone, can't put flowers on his grave. But I know were he is.

One strange thing. Maybe because you were going to interview me. I never dreamt about Gary, *ever*, until a week ago. I think that I was going through the grieving process that day all over again. It was a message to me, "Mom, don't forget me!" I don't. He is in my prayers every night.

These children will never die in their parents' hearts. We shouldn't hold back over the years to mention their names. They have existed.

"Engrave this upon my heart: there isn't anyone you couldn't love once you've heard their story."

—Mary Lou Kownacki, OSB

☎ Compassionate Friends National Office
(For parents who have lost a child)   (708) 990-0010

GENERAL GRIEF

"Grief isn't an enemy that must be conquered; it's an unwelcome visitor that will change your life."

—*Anonymous*

There are many forms of grief. Our first loss is at birth when we arrive helpless in this cold world, separated from our mother. Throughout life when we have temporary feelings of loss or permanent ones we are handed multitudes of clichés. Clichés are the worst enemies of the bereaved, making one's journey through grief more difficult. We need to remember that the bereaved aren't themselves and accept their temporary state of confusion, often using all their energy to maintain their daily functioning. The past is not a slate which can be wiped clean, at will. With time the chalk marks soften, we shouldn't set time limits. Relationships and losses are different — no slide rule.

On this planet of billions of people there are no two people alike. Each one of us is *unique*, we all look and think differently. That's what makes our humanity more valuable.

"When I say 'I,' I mean absolutely unique, not to be confused with any other."

—Unknown

In our present society, grief is considered a waste and an abnormal attitude. It's no longer integrated with life, it's hidden. Some people act like grief is an emotional illness or weakness. Don't bother us with your pain, they seem to say. And what they do say is designed to minimize grief and pain so that they need have no part of it.

Death after an illness:

"At least you had time to say goodbye."
"At least you knew what was happening."
"He is not suffering anymore. It's a blessing. He had suffered so much."
"You must be relieved."
"He is at peace!"
"Your loved one has gone to a better place."

The *best* of the *worst* to a widow, "At least he died! He didn't leave you for another woman."

"God takes the ones he loves the most." Revolting! So, God doesn't love her as much as He loves her husband? And what sadness to be told that God's love causes the loss of loved ones.

"The living *must* go on."

"Get on with your life. You can't continue dwelling on the past."

102

A question asked by one widow of another, "How long were your married?"

"Seventeen years." No sooner was the question answered than the first widow exclaimed, "I was married forty-two years!" Implication, that the second widow's grief should be far less.

Many factors enter into grief for a spouse, kind of marriage, emotional involvement, but not the length of the marriage. Loss isn't measured by time. Time doesn't always make the heart grow fonder. Grief should not be compared, each is *unique*.

"You know, at our age we die! We all have to die sometime." Such comments compound grief.

Some common grief clichés:

After the death of his father a young boy was told, "Now, you are the man of the house. You need to be strong for the others." What a responsibility! And how sad to demand a boy give up his own feelings of loss.

Cliché after sudden death, "At least you didn't watch him suffer!"

To parents whose son died in a motorcycle accident, from their minister,

"God is trying to teach you to be better people."

To another couple whose son died after a short illness, "He might have turned into a criminal." (murder with words)

A man's father died, his friend told him, "He led a long, productive life." Is the friend giving his blessing for the death? No matter how long the father lived, the son has a right to grieve any way he needs to.

Why not say, "You must miss him terribly." Say some kind remark about the father, but with words of concern for the loss. The bereaved need nurturing.

NOTHING makes it right when someone dies.

After ten pre-schoolers were killed in a church van, at the funeral, the minister addressed the parents, "God is testing your faith! Jesus took the children he *wanted* to be with Him!"

Anyone slowly reading these clichés should be appalled. Jesus taking children to test parents' faith is a mockery to His name.

Three women on their way to a club meeting had a car accident, two died. A remark was made to the survivor, "You must have had a guardian angel!" Meaning that the other women died because they didn't have one?

There aren't any *right* words, no formula for caring, but the choice to care can be made; and it's the choice to care that makes the words right.

ENGAGE BRAIN BEFORE SPEAKING

There is no right way to live
no right way to die
no right way to grieve.
Judgement is wasted energy
there are no recipes
no formulas
no pat answers
there is only HOPE.

—*Anonymous*

BELOVED
PET'S DEATH

Rachel is in her mid-fifties with striking reddish hair.

On his third tour of duty in Vietnam, my husband was thrown against the bulkhead of his PT boat during a battle. Because of his injuries the Navy retired him with a disability discharge. He died ten years later. Those were good years, although I spent lots of time in hospital waiting rooms. I called him from work and when I got home, he had the supper ready for me. After he died I couldn't go home after work. I'd go to the mall until the mall closed, then drive around into the wee hours until I had to go home for an hour or two of sleep and get ready for work. It was killing me.

My stepson bought Youki for me, his idea to help me with the loneliness. This little poodle was so tiny, so helpless and totally lovable. Everyday after work, I rushed home to let my baby puppy out, feed her and hold her.

She got me over that terrible feeling of coming home to a completely empty house and empty life. I couldn't face that and, because of Youki, I didn't have to, at least not all at once.

She is nine years old now, really old for a dog. A few months ago, I took her to the vet to have a tumor removed from her jaw. It was cancerous. People, even family members had tried to talk me out of having it done. They told me that I was *crazy* to pay so much to try to save such an old dog. They kept repeating "Youki is so old and *only* a dog."[1] I am retired, the surgery was terribly costly, but I had to try to save my dog's precious life. She had been

---

1   **Author's note:** Individuals who lose their pets do not receive support. They conceal their grief for fear of being ridiculed, real grief not recognized. We need to respect their loss even though we might not understand. People who lose a beloved pet need support. They go through the same stages of anger, disbelief, deep sorrow, depression and most of all loneliness.

Some people have such strong attachments to pets because they can't handle the complexity of human relationships, or because everyday closeness isn't available to them. Pets give unconditional love and can be a life saving presence for the elderly, shut-ins and the handicapped. Also it could have been a couple's pet which remained after the death of one of them, now a double loss.

Immediately replacing a pet after its death often is too traumatic especially if the person lives alone. Discounting the loss with clichés is hurtful, "It was *only* a dog, not human."

Children too should be allowed to grieve the loss of a pet without discounting the death by the cliché, "We'll get you another one." The honest experience of grief can help them with future losses in their lives.

so loving and so important in my life. She has been doing well although I have to feed her soft food because half of her cancerous jaw was removed. She is frisky again and not suffering. She'll be okay for a while longer.

I dread what people will say after she dies. After all Youki is *only* a dog. They won't understand my grief. I don't know how I'd have survived my husband's death if Youki hadn't been there for me.

I wish that people simply wouldn't shower others with clichés after the loss of a loving pet like Youki. People still roll their eyes thinking that I was foolish and insane to have the surgery done.

"Wise sayings often fall on barren ground, but a kind word is never thrown away."

—*Anonymous*

Part 5

ILLNESSES

AIDS

Jerry is in his early forties, personable, well-read and very spiritual. He radiates peace, kindness and concern for others.

My family has a great tradition of not talking about problems. I took my father to an AIDS memorial. I wanted to show him reality. He is very selective on what he wants to see or hear and tunes me out at will. I thought he would have been more understanding. He is not listening, avoiding my sickness. When I told him that I was writing a living will, I got total silence, not animosity, but dread and fear. It was as though my illness didn't exist. He doesn't want to talk about it, not even mention the word AIDS. He only said, "I hope that I will die before you do." It made me very angry.

I went to visit my family in New Orleans. My brothers and sisters told me, "We might not understand, but we still love you." It was a tearful reunion. Families will give you a hug with total silence. They didn't know what to say. Maybe it's better that way.

My brother-in-laws are very homophobic, they were very distant. One did shake my hand. The family was very guarded. I have a niece, an incredible little baby. They always kept her a foot or two away from me. I love children and would have been so happy to hold her. It wasn't worth making an issue of their fear. It did hurt. My sister gave me a cheerful, warm hug that was heartfelt. It is funny how sometimes we compromise ourselves in the interest of peace. I don't hold it against them, I know where they are coming from. It doesn't diminish my love for them. I try not to judge.

A friend with AIDS is still working although he has a T-cell below 100 and his energy level is failing him. His family asked him, "You don't look sick, why are you applying for disability? Why are you going to leave your job? You look well. You should be working." There is no way he can do it. He no longer has the physical stamina to carry it through. He has gone way beyond what is advisable and has already shortened his life due to this stress. His family doesn't see it. They are more concerned about where the money is coming from. Now he feels that he is letting them down which adds a tremendous amount of guilt.

I am annoyed by the stereotype of people with AIDS. People tell me, "You don't look emaciated. You don't look that bad." I want to shake them. Many AIDS sufferers are not in the fourth stage which is terminal. They look like everyday persons. If the majority of people have this attitude, this image of AIDS, they'll think,

"Hey! I can tell." What they aren't realizing is that you can have no symptoms for ten years, all the while contaminating others through sex. It's frightening!

The first reaction when someone finds out that you have AIDS is, "You are gay!" In my case, yes, but it isn't the common denominator. My biggest frustration is lecturing at schools with young males who have a macho attitude. They think AIDS is not their problem. They get argumentive and so self-righteous. It's very hard not to get angry. You need to desensitize yourself if you are to conquer their ignorance. Getting mad doesn't accomplish anything, it just cuts off the dialogue.

A married man tested positive but not his wife and children. They are traumatized, in shock. How did it happen? He is not gay! AIDS has no gender. If the conditions of transmission are met, the disease is transmitted.

Blind fear is the biggest and most curious aspect of AIDS. Men don't want to ask. They think it brings into question their own masculinity. At workshops women ask ninety per cent of the questions, real ones. Women are very aware of what is going on. After my presentations, some men will ask questions — privately. They won't speak in front of others.

I get angry when I do presentations for religious groups. I can't use the words semen or penis. How did we all end up being conceived? It's a mystery.

Even in the gay community there is a lot of discrimination, lots of ignorance and malicious talk. "You know so and so. He has AIDS." As if they were above reproach.

They are often the ones who don't want to be tested. They are afraid.

At hospitals we only ask to be treated with kindness. When a friend's lover dies I call to see if there is anything I can do. We all breathe, speak, eat, talk, walk. We need to love and be loved, give, share, be all we can be. We all have our own sensitivities. Some people are so petty saying, "What are you upset about?" You can't understand or even identify with the situation. Allow them to be upset. *I know how you feel.* You never really can.

Since I have been diagnosed with AIDS, it made me ask, "Why am I here? What is my purpose?" Life is so fleeting. I am trying to do things that will make the most difference with the time I have left.

"I am only one; but still I am one. I cannot do everything, but still I can do something. I will not refuse to do something I can do."

—*Helen Keller*

☎ AIDS hotline   (800) 342-2437

ARTHRITIS

During the interview with Ruth, I was fascinated with her positive outlook on life. She has arthritis. She leads a very constructive life — helping others in similar circumstances.

Some very embarrassing incidents happened to me before my surgery. My hands and feet were deformed. One day standing in line at a grocery store a child wanted to know why my hands and feet looked so funny. The mother tried to shush him to keep him from asking questions. If she had let him, I could have told the child that my hands and feet were deformed by a sickness called arthritis. He would have learned something. Parental attitudes are handed down to their children.

Another time I was walking on a sidewalk. Some children passing by were looking, pointing and giggling. My little girl, who at that time was in second grade turned around, planted her feet and said, "Don't you stare at my mother. Don't you know it's not nice!"

People have no idea how CRUEL some words are. The word *crippled* is very hurtful and I don't like the *tic* at the end of words like: arthri-*tic* or epilep-*tic*. They hurt my ears because they are hard-sounding words. People don't like *chronic* diseases. They are not something you can fix and it goes away. Being incurable they're lifetime.

Other hurtful words are *victim*, *sufferer* and *deformed*. Sometimes such words can be used as adjectives. As an example before her surgery she had *deformed* feet. You are not saying, *she is deformed*. *She* is first a person, that changes the whole connotation.

At airports, because distances are so great I always use a wheelchair. My daughter usually takes me to the gate. One time, the agent, ready to preboard me, asked my daughter, "Can she walk to the bathroom?" Just because I have to use a wheelchair doesn't mean that my brain doesn't function and that I can't talk. I try to laugh, but it still hurts. I try to block out what people say and do. It's not easy.

It makes all the difference on board when a flight attendant offers to cut your meat, break a roll or open cellophane packages. When you ask for help some show by their attitude and body language that they would rather not. Some jerk the packages open, one actually refused to help. Learning to ask for help was a very tough thing for me to master.

At a lecture on arthritis I was sitting next to a man and before it started we chatted. He asked, "You drive?"

It is hard to ignore people's unthoughtful remarks. Of course, why shouldn't I? I am a good driver.

One day I went with my son to a discount store to buy tires. A woman kept pushing one of those large flatbed carts in front of me. She wanted to tell me about a cure for arthritis. She stated that I should go to a certain place and take this mysterious medication. She almost physically accosted me. Finally, she put the flatbed across the aisle so I wouldn't be able to pass. I had to tell her that I would call a security guard if she didn't leave me alone.

Not long after that incident, a woman in a drugstore accosted me, "You have to try Dr. So and So's magic medicine." It happened again in a restaurant's restroom while my husband and I were touring southern Texas. After I was there a while he started to worry. He sent a woman to see if I was all right. Another woman had followed me and wanted me to drive with her across the border at Laredo. She was practically holding me hostage. She was so sure that her Mexican cure would heal me. Even though well-intentioned, I have had some frightening experiences. I try to be patient, but at times it gets to be scary and too much.

Aspirin ads on TV and radio each claiming they are the greatest relief for *minor* arthritis pain and aches. People used to think *just* take two aspirins; in my case that's not true. This drives me crazy. When you've lived with arthritis for nineteen years and I've gone through pain all these years, it makes me so angry and I wanted to throw my TV through the window. There is nothing *minor* about pain with my disability. It's a wrong attitude.

People do die from complications and arthritis shortens life expectancy.

Some people are afraid of offering assistance because they don't know what to do. They only have to ask. I'd rather hang on to somebody than to have someone squeeze my hand too tight and hurt it. Those who need help should make people aware of the kind we need. It's a dual responsibility from the person who needs help and the person who wants to help.

I went to a Bible study group. We prayed at the end of each session. One young woman told me that I wasn't being healed because I didn't have any faith and didn't believe in God. I tried to tell her that I was healed inside and resented her questioning *my* relationship with *my* God. In all those years this incident caused the DEEP-EST hurt because it is a place one doesn't trespass. Help me across the street, up steps, out of a chair but don't mess around with *my* relationship with *my* God. At times it's okay to get angry when people are overly inconsiderate.

We have to take responsibilities for ourselves and our well-being and make ourselves function the best we can. Sometimes we feel that we have to be superhuman in order to prove that we can do what other people do.

People with sicknesses and disabilities are human like anyone else, some of us have parts which do not work very well. Each person has to be taken separately—our chemistries, reactions or lack of them are different. We want to do the things we can do well just like anyone else wants to. It is better to think of similarities than differences. I have a disease and you a disorder. We both drive cars, do grocery shopping, attend social occasions and enjoy them.

We are more alike than different. The only difference is that we had to learn to live with our disabilities. You and I can change people's attitudes and we have that responsibility.

The rest of the world is crazy except you and me. Certainly we need to have a sense of humor or we'll never make it.

"Laugh at yourself and you'll always be entertained."

—*Chinese proverb*

☎ Arthritis Foundation   (800) 283-7800

CANCER

Jeanne is a pretty middle-age woman with a winning smile. She wears her black hair in an attractive pixie style.

Breast cancer is every woman's nightmare.

People often tell me, "You are a fighter." Maybe I am. Maybe I don't want to be. They try to tell me what I am, but they are not me. Others say, "You can do it."

I was telling a friend that I had just come back from a doctor's appointment. He had told me that the cancer had spread. Of all things, she suggested that I tell the doctor that this was just not acceptable. What the doctor had told me was reality, and I was to tell him that the truth was not acceptable! Really!

Recently someone said, "It seems that all you do with your life is taking chemo treatments. That's all you are doing. I sure hope that *stuff* is going to do what it is supposed to do." The way *stuff* was said made it sound awful.

Very few people understand why I needed to be in the hospital during four days for the treatment. They wanted to know why I couldn't have it done at home! Those four days are getting harder and harder. It feels like a month. My wish is that I could do something. They could have instead said, "Chemo is good and often works. I hope it will be beneficial for you." A simple statement doesn't ask for advice, but it comes! It brings so much. The litany starts:

I don't understand why you don't walk around the hospital.
I don't understand why you don't read or watch TV.
I don't understand why you don't call friends.

During my chemo treatments people can't understand that my mind gets muddled and I can't concentrate. It seems everyone has answers for me. What I should do now and how. THEY ARE NOT ME! I didn't ask for advice, *please* just listen.

What has helped a lot are the prepared meals that you have organized for a week after my return from the hospital. It has helped a lot as I was too weak to cook. My husband works long hours.

Once when I got a cold a woman told me, "You mean to tell me you are going to be down for five days!" I do what my doctor tells me, not what everyone else thinks I should do. They don't understand and don't even try.

People have told my son that they don't call or come around because they don't know what to say. I have even lost friends because I have cancer. It helps me to talk about it. I very seldom bring it up except with a few old trusted friends. Why can't we talk about what we used to talk about, children, recipes or world affairs. When I meet someone in a grocery store I would like them to talk about food, or ordinary things. I do the same things that everybody does. Don't treat me as if I have a label marked CANCER. You don't have to say anything about my sickness or make empty remarks, "You look good. You are a fighter. The medicine must be working." Just FORGET IT! I am labeled, I feel victimized because society feels the need to say something to me about illness. I am cancer, nothing, nobody. Just say whatever anybody would say when they meet another person. Naturally it's okay to ask. "How are you doing." I say that to anybody. *I am still alive!*

I don't think they know you can see the fear written all over their faces. I have been facing death, but the world doesn't want to talk about it. They are afraid of facing their own mortality.

It would be nice to have a conversation just like you and I are doing. We can openly discuss cancer, my lack of fear of death. People need to be open about it. If the conversation turns toward my illness, people shouldn't feel compelled to stop. I would like to explore and get other people's ideas about cancer. The whole thing is sad.

It's very hard when people make promises you know they won't keep. A casual friend said, "We found a real neat little restaurant. We'll take you." I'd much rather they didn't say a thing than have them give me empty promises.

A classic one, "I've been meaning to visit you in the hospital and see you." Then all the meaningless excuses follow. Only empty words. I see guilt written all over their faces. They wish they had not run into me.

My biggest fear is the quality of my death. I am working on changing my life because it is said that if you have inner peace, love and joy inside you, you will die peacefully with love and joy. The hardest thing for me is leaving my earthly ties — my husband and children. I hope that I will be with them in spirit so that when they have to make important decisions I will be part of them.

"A kind word is like a spring day."

—Russian proverb

☎ American Cancer Society   (800) ACS-2345

HEART
DISEASE

Robert is a former high profile executive of an invest-ment firm located on the east coast. He is a jolly, short man with blond hair mixed with white.

In 1989 I started having signs of maybe heart trouble. It went on for about a year. In the fall, my wife was in the hospital for observation. While visiting her, our family doctor dropped in to see her. As he was leaving he said, "I should take a look at you. I haven't seen you in a year or more." After the physical he suggested that I see a cardiologist. I followed his advice. The doctor found that I had a complete blockage at the right end side of my heart, and almost complete blockage on the left. He wasn't sure how come I was still walking. How my heart disease was detected was quite a fluke.

My work as a key manager of a corporation didn't seem to affect me any, but I ended up in surgery, quadruple bypass. After such surgery one can become a cripple if you allow it to be. People who are aware of my problem don't want me to lift anything.

When we come out of rehab (rehabilitation), we know our limitations. I can pick up a glass and have three people tell me, "Let me carry that for you. You might hurt yourself." Let me decide if I can carry it or not. They have to understand that I am the one who decides what I can or can't lift. I'll let them know if I want somebody to help me. They do it to this day.

After such a surgery one goes through a series of major life changes. I was a very lucky man. At that time I was fifty-three years old. Still had a lot of vigor and was not ready to cash it in. Corporations don't always look at it that way nor do people.

On account of the surgery I lost my job. After less than nine months I was asked to leave. I naturally asked if it was poor performance. The answer was they were afraid that with my kind of problem I wouldn't be able to be a key performer, and "we don't think we can put you any place else in the company and really do us any good." They threw me to the wolves. Fifty-three years old. It is kind of frightening. Suddenly you are out in the street.

They were very nice, great severance package which does not help a bit as far your feelings go. It helped the wallet but it sure didn't one's self-esteem. I actually was put out to pasture. Their thinking was they couldn't have a key manager with this kind of medical problems. They didn't know at what point I might kick the bucket, or

123

have a heart attack. You are injured. You have a problem.
You are gone. It is a little known fact that people like me
are a threat to employers and more so in management
positions.

After that I started researching my rights. My lawyer
said, "We probably can take this to court, but we wouldn't
win. You have to understand that people are pretty much
ignorant about these things. If you really knew what
happens behind all these decisions, you'd be surprised."
After seeing a couple of attorneys I gave up. It wasn't
worth my effort to file a suit. I found out from one of the
company's secretaries that the reason for my release was
the company insurance rates went up. It wasn't because
I might drop dead at a board meeting, but because of the
insurance rates. I thought, it's amazing, one can put in
a lot of years with a company and their only concern is
their *purse*.

I came out of the surgery real well, went through the
exercise program. Because there wasn't any real heart
damage I really bounced back real quick. But I had real
psychological problems getting adjusted. My problem was
that my mind didn't accept my body's condition. Heart
patients normally go through some depression. The depth
varies, mine was called medium.

I was sent to see a nurse, Ruth Wagner at DES
(Department of Economic Security). She specialized in
cardiac cases and handled many of them like mine. Many
young men in their forties couldn't get a job. She was the
greatest person, helping her patients find jobs and even
lodging. What I sensed about her and what surprised me,

was that she was very empathic to our problems. She became a friend.

Ruth sent me to see a psychologist. He really worked with me. He told me that I was too young to cash it in. "Let's go on to do something else," he said. After a couple of sessions he told me, "Why don't you start your own business? You don't have to work for somebody else. You don't want to go back in the corporate world to be squeezed out again. If you do, we'll have you right back in the hospital. Your stress level can't take it." He was very encouraging. I thought he was crazy, because having your own business must be stressful. He added, "You'll find out that *you* will have control of what goes on. When you are in control, you body and mind knows that. You'll handle it. It is a different type of stress. Not damaging." It has proven true.

Ruth asked me to go to a local disability fair. A couple things happened there that really opened my eyes. One comment was about a different career, "You are not even in a wheelchair!" from a person at a display table. I don't know that I have a total disability? I have a problem, I have heart disease. It will never go away. How I handle it is something else. It's always going to be there. It doesn't show. I don't need a walker or a wheelchair. I thought it was a thoughtless statement.

The next one happened when petition signatures were solicited for the Americans with Disabilities Act, a great one I thought. I stopped at the booth. Right away I was asked to sign, "What am I signing?"

"It's a petition to get the disability act passed."

She gave me some literature, mostly about wheelchair access. "What about people like me?" I wanted to know.

"What's wrong with you?"

"I just had major heart surgery a year ago and lost my job."

"You aren't considered in this disability act. It is for people with special needs in getting around. You get around just fine."

"Then, I don't want to sign your petition. I might want to have it reworded because you don't understand my problems."

A lady came to separate us because things were getting a little bit hot. I didn't sign the petition. The disability act was a good one, but not extensive enough. Didn't clear the ignorance. People are still very unaware of what happens when a person is disabled.

I was very lucky after that to get into a business of my own. During all that time I attended a support group called *Mended Hearts*. They came and visited me when I was in the hospital. I was very impressed with what they had to say. Later I became a member, it was my turn to visit heart patients in hospitals. We visit during and after they leave the hospital. We try to dispel some of the patients' fears. Doctors and hospitals are behind what we do. Younger male patients in general are ignorant about what happens with heart disease. One young man I thought was never going to leave the hospital. He kept saying, "My life is over. I lost my job. My wife called my former employers regarding vacation pay. When she went to pick up it up, my things were boxed up, sitting in the hallway. What do I have to live for?"

I answered, "You have a couple of nice kids in the waiting room." They were fairly young. "That's one of the reasons you might want to fight the idiots. If you get out and get yourself rehabilitated, get your mind in the right place. You have a whole life ahead of you." People live a long time with heart disease. It used to be when a person went through a similar operation there was a five to six year life expectancy. Now with medication there isn't a time limit. Heart operations have been perfected. Now patients listen, make corrections in their lifestyle. That's a big improvement factor.

I still to this day, *ten* years later run into the stigmas. If people see me visiting someone in the hospital, it's time to beware! "You are one of them," that's their attitude. I'm there to help a fellow heart patient get well, out of the hospital and get back to his life, but I've even heard the limiting concept from nurses and doctors. They get a little nervous sometimes and we've had the same debate on how disabling heart disease should be. One doctor had told a patient that he probably would have to give up his job. He was a young fellow.

With the families there are a lot of different feelings. We patients get wrapped up in ourselves. You get some resentment from your spouses. I understand my wife's thoughts. There were times not long after my surgery she could not sleep. She was afraid I wouldn't wake up in the morning. She would check me regularly making sure I was still breathing. That created some problems. Spouses, either gender, go through the various stages of reactions like us, denial that there's anything wrong. Now it's okay, it's healed up, we can forget about it. It will never happen again. That's our biggest one particularly with the males when they are dependent on the wife to fix meals, make sure to keep them on their dietary track. You are now walking around, things are great, let's get back to steak and potatoes. Patients must learn to say, "No. Let's stay on the prescribed diet."

Part of rehab is a visit with a nutritionist. Mine worked very hard at getting the meals set up. She is the one who allowed me to have some fun. She said the biggest problem they have is working with spouses. The diets are difficult and forever and ever. We can't have those arteries clog up again.

Our only daughter didn't seem to want to understand. Ten years later she keeps on asking, "You sure you are all right. You are not working too many hours? Shouldn't you be easing up a little bit." I am the one to judge if I should do so or not. I appreciate her concern, *but* it gets annoying. One of my two sons lives in town. He is very understanding. If I ask for his help with my business or home he never questions why. I know my limitations. I will not climb on the roof carrying tools. The hardest part is for others to understand my decisions, and let me decide.

In many cases people say stupid things. One neighbor asked, "Why didn't you put your Christmas lights up?" I had been operated on in November. Annoyed I answered, "I don't feel comfortable climbing that ladder yet."

He added, "I saw you walking the other day. I assumed that everything was okay." I don't plan to go around with a sign stating I have some limitations on what I do.

When we are out with friends it never fails that one will say, "Oh! Come on have a T-bone, it won't hurt you. Have a baked potato. Have that drink, it won't hurt you." They don't know what that one drink or potato will do. The situation involves the reactions to my medication. Not the same stress!

I am also constantly asked if I still drive....

After a year wandering around doing consulting work I ended with my own graphic business. It's successful.

"Suffering isn't ennobling, recovery is."

—*Christian N. Barnard, M.D.*

☎ National Heart Association   (314) 373-6300

HODGKIN'S DISEASE

*J*oan *is a nurse in a San Francisco hospital. She is a cute twenty-six, vivacious young woman with an inquiring mind. What differentiates her from others is a large horizontal scar on her throat under her chin. I had met her on a plane. As I told her about my book on clichés she related some rather annoying ones.*

When I was nine years old I had Hodgkin's disease. After the biopsy I was given three days to live. I lay in a coma for a month and a half. That ordeal was followed by radiation. During the treatments I was told not to move because if I did the machine would cut me. I was terrified, it made it all the more difficult.

During those days I was always called a miracle child. It bothered me. Since then, I feel that I owe the world something, that I am not accomplishing enough to pay back. I am an overachiever.

My type of cancer was always kept hushed. I hated people asking, "Are you getting better?" Everyone expects your body to function right, too soon. It was frustrating. I was also told, "Look at what other people have, some are worse than you." I didn't want to look at what other people had. I needed to concentrate on myself to get better. After the chemo my parents were very protective. I stayed home, watched TV and gained weight. People would say, "She has a cute face, a dimple, but she needs to lose weight." I was called FAT and FATSO. At that time my weight was my sense of security. I felt so alone.

Because of the chemo treatments I can't have children. Since then I have been saturated with clichés, "Maybe you were not meant to have children or weren't supposed to experience motherhood."

"You can always adopt."
"At least you are alive."

How I hate this last one and its absurd implications.

People ask me if I am married. When I say *no*, invariably the come back is, "You are so pretty, you should get married, get pregnant and live barefoot." Funny! Or, "You are too young to be a nurse and care for cancer patients." Were they implying that I am unable to give good care because I am youthful?

Why must they *say* these hurtful clichés without bothering to think?

When people notice the scar it rarely fails to inspire unreasonable questions. Questions, questions...questions...

"Did you try to commit suicide?"
"Did you have thyroid surgery?"
"What did you do?"
"What happened? Are you okay?"
"Is it bothering you?"
"Why don't you get plastic surgery?"

And the worst, "It's a pretty big hickey." How gross!
For years I walked with my head down, until one day a man told me, "Look up to the sky. It's so beautiful. Stand tall." He left me with a positive thought that I think of often. I am grateful for his encouraging words. Instead of clichés, empty words, he did me a favor with encouraging, positive words.

"The center of human nature is rooted in ten thousand ordinary acts of kindness that define our days."

"A truth that's told with bad intent beats all the lies you can invent."

—*William Blake, Auguries of Innocence*

☎ American Cancer Society   (800) ACS-2345

LUPUS

Jenny is in her forties. Small boned with striking long back hair. She lives alone in an apartment complex.

More than three million people suffer from lupus, many have not been diagnosed because it can take years before the disease can be pinpointed. Some are mild cases, others severe. Lupus is a chronic disease which causes inflammation of various parts of the body. The immune system gets overactive, it attacks its own body. More people are afflicted with lupus than AIDS.

Lupus causes inflammation of the joints, and especially the skin causing rashes. Blood and kidneys can also be affected. The whole results in many complications. It comes and goes, flares up for a week, months or years and then it's gone. Most people have never heard of lupus, others don't know what it is.

My body is rejecting my own tissues, attacking the joints. That's where the pain comes from. Women between the age of fifteen and forty-five, women in child bearing years are the most susceptible. But some as young as seven have been diagnosed up to the nineties. Men get lupus also, often at puberty.

I was diagnosed when I was twenty-two during my last year in a small Iowa college. During the following ten years I was off my medication only for one year. At the present I feel pretty good.

That summer I went to Europe then I ended up having trouble again. When I was first diagnosed I was very ill. The symptoms were a lot of pain. Some mornings I would get up and not be able to move my hands, knees, have severe back pain, and I hurt everywhere. I woke up stiff, couldn't walk, then it would take me two to three hours to start functioning. All these years I have had a low grade fever in the morning, by five o'clock in the afternoon and, even if I don't do anything, it will go up to 102° or 103°. The pain gets worse and I *have* to take pain pills. I can function until the fever is more than 100 degrees, then I need to take something.

In my last year of college, I had been sick and at that time it was unexplained. I had very high grades, and was in the honor society I was doing student teaching with Sally, a teacher who had a drinking problem. She would leave during the day and expect me to cover up for her, take the class. When I got sick she got very upset. Halfway through the semester I found out what was wrong with me — lupus, I had to leave. I didn't know much about lupus. My parents thought I would die because my father knew someone who had died of the disease.

134

When I told Sally the diagnosis she uncaringly said, "Oh! Are you going to be here with me for the rest of the school term or die?"

I answered, "Well, I hope that I make it until the end of the year. I'll try."

After graduating from college, I taught the first year, and did very well until the very last week. I took the kids out, got sunburnt. I knew better, but was in denial then. The following day I could not move, one side was almost paralysed. The summer went by, I taught one week of the fall classes, got sick again, and missed the whole year. I was so huge then, humongous. The school janitor asked if I was pregnant!

It was devastating to be told that I could not stay in the sun. In college, I used to love sunbathing a lot. Could not believe that the sun had become my worst enemy. If I stayed in the sun I'd get a bad headache and be nauseous. When I go out I need to cover myself completely. Now I no longer take chances with my enemy.

I had to tell my pupils that I was on chemotherapy and that's why I missed classes. Most of the children showed compassion. Two set of parents went to the school board asking them to remove their children from my class because they had heard that lupus was contagious. There was a big fight with the school board. When I found out I was devastated. Another couple went to see the principal because they were afraid I would die before the end of the school year. It would be too traumatic for their child.

I know that I will have this disease for the rest of my life. Sometimes I can't do stuff and have to stay in bed, naked with only a sheet over me. I get very depressed. It isn't worth getting up. Treatments wiped me out.

My mother had a hard time understanding my deep depressions. I took medication for my mood swings. My father was cynical. He didn't want me to do volunteer work. If you do, he said, you won't be able to buy another car. He wanted me to make money. At the beginning of my illness I complained all the time. I was miserable, the queen of self-pity. When I stopped complaining my parents decided I was better, must be okay, doing real good. Then when I took my pain pills they would say, "Why are you taking those for?"

I remember not being compassionate toward over-weight people, telling my family,

"If I ever get fat, kick me!"

At one time I gained a 100 pounds. I was always very vain about my appearance and weight. With my beautiful jet black hair and good looks, I received a lot of attention. I progressed from pretty to ugly. Because I was so huge, my eyes were slits, my mouth swollen. When I went places, people were scared of me and pointed. Sometimes I would sweat terribly, I would be dripping and have to go home to take a shower.

The mirror was my worst enemy.... Because of gaining weight so fast, I had purple, ugly stretch marks all the way down to my ankles. Some became so huge that I could put two fingers in the stretch marks. I have gone back and forth in my weight.

One day I went to the doctor's office, sat down in the waiting room. A woman got up and moved her children to the other side of the waiting room. Her little daughter said, "What's wrong with you? Why don't you take a bath?"

It was just a bad rash. I was so embarrassed, it was so very difficult. The first year was extremely frustrating.

At one time I had a boyfriend, we were engaged to be married. We lived together. Even though his mother had died of lupus when he was young, he didn't know much about the disease. I was so afraid of being fat and ugly that I started to lose my confidence and self-esteem. James used to tell me that he didn't care how big I would get as long as I did the best I could.

I hated shopping, stayed home wearing old stuff. But one day I needed groceries. At the store the female store manager told the cashier that I wore the same old clothes every day because I was so fat. It was so embarrassing that I left and cried all the way home. People are so hurtful, and really, she could have been kinder. If she wanted to talk about me, do it after I was gone and not when I could hear her.

After that incident, I went to a store to buy a nice dress that fit me, size 26 or 28. I went home, cleaned the house, did my hair, used makeup, and put the dress on. I was so proud of myself, I didn't look that bad. James came home from work, walked in, looked me up and down, said, "Gosh, you gained more weight!"

I crashed. Disgusted I went to my room saying, "Forget it." I took everything off.

James would say horrible things like that to me all the time. He worked in the headquarters of a large real estate company, the corporate world. He had always enjoyed having a pretty woman at his arm. When I started changing, he was embarrassed at my appearance. He made excuses why I should not go to this or that function. I found out later that at work he was telling his co-workers that we no longer lived together. So many things he said and did destroyed my confidence completely. He looked at me, he would shake his head. It wasn't my fault.

Every time I start eating he would say, "Do you really need that? Are you going to eat that much? I don't know what to do, you are gaining all that weight."

I was not gaining it on purpose. My weight gain was my worst nightmare. He was not consoling me, but was adding to my sense of worthlessness. When I started standing up for myself and complaining because I was sick, he would leave and not come home until the next day.

At one point he reproached me for complaining about his staying out all night. He told me that I was *lucky* he was letting me live with him. Adding that most people would have taken a hike by now because I had become so ugly and so sick. I had *no* right to complain, *no* right to want anything because *no* one would ever love me again or stay with me. If it was not for him I would not have a life, he said. At that time I believed it and I was really frightened that *no* one in the world would want to take on such a mess!

We decided to go for counseling. In front of the therapist's he acted like he was the *good* one, but at home he was the opposite.[1]

---

1   **Author's note:** Verbal domestic violence is very detrimental.

I started having trouble with my feet. My toes started turning purple and black followed by blisters. No longer could I walk, someone would have to come and get me with a car. I went to my primary doctor, "Have you tried water aerobics?" she asked.

"I am not worried about exercising at the present," I answered, "only about walking."

"You are not going to be able to walk anymore. If it hurts, don't walk!" How callous!

Angrily I told her, "I want to be able to walk around the house, and to my car without my cane."

"I'll send you to see a podiatrist."

Being on HMO I could not get an appointment until TWO months later!

People think that if your disease is not life threatening, you shouldn't worry. It makes me so angry that I end up crying.

After the foot surgery I was in a wheelchair for six months. During that time James charged my credit cards to the limit. Without my knowledge he bought a house, furnished it.

One day I got a call from a major department store's accounts receivable office stating that my bill was overdue. I was livid, and told the woman, "Wait awhile. I am very sick, soon I'll be dead and you can collect from my estate."

"Honey, what's the good of living if you don't have credit?" That was a doozy! A good one!

I had a lot of trouble with my temporary handicap plates on my car. After the surgery on my feet my problems started because I had casts on my legs for six months. One day a man rolled down his window yelling, "I hate people who take advantage of handicap spaces."

When I came out on crutches he said, "Oh! I am sorry," then left.

The sessions with the counselor were not helping, so I finally used my brains and left James. I moved to New Mexico. I didn't want handicap plates because I was so young and didn't want anyone asking me what my problem was.

The problem is that *I don't look sick*. I use my handicap sign only when I need it. One day after my hip replacement I went to a park to watch a friend play softball. I parked in a handicap spot because general parking was far, left the car after hanging the temporary sign on the rear view mirror. Park employees came over telling me that I looked fine, and that I was abusing the space. They threatened to call the police stating that they would give me a ticket.

Angrily, I said, "You don't know what you are talking about. I am handicapped. Go ahead, call them."

The police did come, got me out of the bleachers. One policeman asked for my handicap papers. Furiously I told him, "I own this car. It's none of your business what's wrong with me. I am legally allowed to park here. You have no right to see the paper work. I want your badge number."

He answered, "You don't look handicapped, why are you taking this space?"

Finally I turned around, pulled up my shorts up over my butt. "Look, I am plastic from here to here."

They left. Why did I have to go through this ordeal?

Another time at a mall a construction worker yelled, "Handicap signs mean physically handicapped, not mentally, nor stupid, fat and ugly. Handicapped, period!"

It was so embarrassing, I felt so bad, discouraged and dejected.

Seems that most of my problems with people happened in parking lots. Some time later, after I parked, a man walking by with a cane started hitting the top of my car with his cane, "You want to be handicapped?" he asked. Eventually I got the handicap plates, the harassment continued but to a lesser degree. Most of the time I would answer, "It's none of your business."

I didn't want to be rude, but how I wanted to yell, scream at them, "Can't you be kind? Can't you leave me alone?"

I understand somewhat because I don't look sick. Believe me, I earned that handicap plate. Trust me, I earned it, I earned it!

Of all places at a church parking lot a woman said, "You don't look sick..." but as soon as I got my cane and walker out of the car, she turned beet red. Disgusted I angrily told her because I was fed up, "Sorry that I don't limp." I ended apologizing that I didn't meet her requirements.

When I got sick, my best friend turned on me, accusing me of being a hypochondriac. "Knock it off," she said. "There is nothing wrong with you."

Some medications have horrible side effects. When I felt bad, I would call her hoping for some moral support. Instead she would say, "Why are you taking that stuff?"

"Because I prefer not to die. Medicine you call *stuff* is saving my life."

"Who told you that? You are not going to die. Why do you keep saying that. I don't know who ever told you that? Don't take that stuff if it makes you feel so bad."

It was like telling me that I was an idiot.

I started lecturing on lupus and when I mentioned the disease people would say,

"Oh! You have lupus, I am so sorry. When are you going to die?" or "I knew someone with lupus. She died. I am sorry."

A lot of hurtful remarks are made by doctors. Many think they are *gods*. They don't understand. A good doctor if he doesn't have enough knowledge will admit it and suggest seeing another one. But my doctor did such a wonderful job on my hip.

At my ten-year high school reunion, people told me that I *should* lose weight, *should* exercise. All those *shoulds*! It is difficult to exercise on account of the pain. If I do, I am finished for the rest of the day because I only have a certain amount of energy. While I was attending a party, an acquaintance started to talk about the Social Security system and how so many people abuse it. "They need to get rid of the whole system." he advised anyone within earshot. Without thinking I said, "I am on disability, without social security, the medical care, I wouldn't survive. I would die."

Astounded he replied, "*You*! *You* on disability!"

"Yes. You know that I can't work. How do you think I get along?"

"I didn't know you are *one of those people*! You are not sick, you look *fine*."

"You know I am not well inside, that I have been very sick. Every time I try to work I get worse and the disease gets worse each time. Eventually it will kill me."

Condescendingly he asked, "And, what do you do all day long?"

"When I feel good I give my time to the Lupus Foundation, I do volunteer work, and..."

Without letting me go any further, he interrupted, "If you volunteer, you can work. That's my whole point. If you volunteer, why don't you find a place which pays for what you do."

"You don't understand," I replied. "When I feel better, I only volunteer for a few hours a week, sometimes or more, but it might be followed by six months when I am unable to do anything. If you can find me a job I can do, which will pay me enough to cover my medical insurance let me know. I'll take that job tomorrow." I was so hurt and humiliated that I left the party.

Someone else made a very hurtful remark,

"If I was sick like you, I would kill myself."

Recently, I have not had a flare up, the last one was when I was still with James and at that time in a wheelchair. Shows what stress can do to the body. I have this bastard out of my life now.

I was told by someone that my illness was a *GIFT*. What a twisted mind! At that time I wanted to say, get out, get away from me. Such an attitude is so harmful.

My volunteer work with the Lupus Foundation, working with kids gives me a reason to get up in the morning and it helps a lot. I didn't know who I was. I have come a long, long way. Many times I didn't know if I wanted to live or die.

"Everything becomes possible by the mere presence of someone who knows how to listen, to live and to give of themselves."

—*Elie Weisel, Nobel Prize winner*

☎ **Lupus Foundation of America   (800) 558-0121**

MULTIPLE SCLEROSIS

Maria is a high school teacher who can now only work part-time or substitute. She has two girls thirteen and nine. She lives on Cape Cod.

When people first find out, they always say, "Gee, Maria you look so GOOD!" They want to see something, a sign of the sickness. The body doesn't always reflect what you feel inside. When I went back to teaching, my colleagues said, "You look better than before you got sick!" I started functioning on a level that seemed okay, they assumed I would be back to business as usual. As long as MS doesn't interfere with my teaching, I can go on.

Before I was actually diagnosed, the word *lazy* kept coming up all the time. My husband, Will, who teaches PE, constantly talked about the things that I was putting off. I was lazy, unmotivated and not ambitious. Even though

I was going to the doctor trying to find out what was wrong, many friends kept saying, "You must be depressed."

After all these years, that word is still implanted. There is a fine line between being lazy and working to my full capacity.

Another side effect of multiple sclerosis is forgetfulness. Will gets upset. It isn't that I want to forget. It is due to the part of the brain that has the lesion. He will tell me something and maybe tomorrow I will have forgotten. "I told you that yesterday," Will would snap at me. I didn't mean to forget. It comes up all the time. I feel embarrassed, drained and frustrated. You have to accept what happens to you. Life goes on. The clock can't be reversed.

Fatigue is sometimes brought on by the rise in body temperature. Will and I fight about the thermostat setting. People with MS don't tolerate heat well. He doesn't like cold temperatures and during the winter he is constantly putting the heat up. It was hard trying to get through to him that I wasn't being obnoxious and stubborn, but it is due to my illness. At times we still have trouble with that issue. He thinks like everyone else that if I lay down my body would cool off. It remains the same.

I go over and above what the doctor tells me to do. People forget very fast just how sick you really are because you *do* look well. You can't keep on explaining over and over. It gets old very fast. Because nothing shows, we are expected to function like everyone else.

When I am really down I have been told, "At least it's not cancer! You are not going to die!" How can they be so insensitive and casual. Those are very devastating and disturbing comments. The fact that it's not cancer doesn't help me. Comparing with another illness doesn't take away my pains. They don't understand how upsetting it is to have no future to bank on. You never know what tomorrow will bring.

In the beginning I was very sick. I had a hard time walking around and functioning. I was told, "Why don't you smile? Smiles make you feel better." It took everything I had to be up and moving around, and dealing with my family. It troubled me very much.

When people see me real bad they are usually compassionate. When I am back on my feet, compassion goes by the wayside.

My children are still in denial, they can't understand what I am dealing with. One day I was sick, my oldest wanted me to bake her favorite dessert. I couldn't. The girls are sometimes resentful of the things they have to do. It infringes on their lives. Their attitude really hurts. They know that I have MS, but they'd rather believe that it's not happening to their mom.

MS had disrupted our lives and made some friends very uncomfortable. Many won't talk about it and stay away. I prefer no comments on my illness rather than to listen to clichés.

When I walk with my cane it is obvious that I am not feeling well. I have had people tell me, "I hope you don't drive when you don't see real well." When I am in an episode I don't drive. I have enough sense and know when I can or cannot. I would never endanger myself or others. I am an adult woman. That overbearing question shouldn't be asked. I have better sense than one of my pupil's father who had a massive heart attack behind the wheel. No one had ever asked him if he drove. He had not been taking his medication regularly.

I have a disability sticker on my car which I use only when I really have to. One especially hot day, I parked in an handicapped spot. As I came out of the car a man stopped me and asked, "And what is your affliction?" I was so angry. What gave him the right to ask me such a personal question? Because I looked well? It was degrading. Why should he meddle in my affairs? I felt tense and resented the need to defend myself.

When I am with Will, he decides for me if I am bad enough or not to use a handicap space. He'll park in one when I am with my walker but not when I use my cane. He feels that the handicapped spaces are for wheelchair users. He doesn't feel that my affliction deserves that kind of service.

Only a person with a sickness or disorder can understand another one. MS touches almost every part of one's life. It affects your major muscles movements which are badly deteriorated, and it doesn't show. One important point is that people think that you make more of the illness than it really deserves.

Our society makes a fetish of fitness which causes people to turn away from anyone who doesn't fit the perfect mold.

"The tongue is to be feared more than the sword."

—*Japanese Proverb*

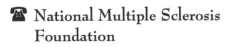 National Multiple Sclerosis
Foundation   (212) 986-3240

CAREGIVERS

Caregivers are frequently so preoccupied with their tasks that they ignore their own physical, mental, emotional and spiritual needs. As the caregiving demands increase, their energy drains.
— *Father Bailey, in CARETAKERS, the Forgotten People*

Lois is a very articulate woman. She is in her sixties, but doesn't look her age.

Home care often imposes emotional, physical strain and often financial burdens which can be overwhelming. Caring for a parent is cause for major stress. It is more taxing than most people think. It requires medical skills that most family caregivers can't perform, especially for a bedridden family member.

A man caring for his father was told, "It will make you stronger!"

What people don't realize unless they have cared for aged parents is that it's a full time job much like raising your children. Only an adult you are caring for is more unpredictable than your children were. You never know from day to day what kind of a mood your parent is going to be in. You exchange roles back and forth, some days you are the child and some days you are the parent to your parent. Often times the parent will forget that you are an adult and you have been on your own for a long period of time. They want to treat you like a child and tell you what to do. Sometimes they are very, very dependent and you are definitely the parent. It can be very trying, very draining because you are on the job full time. You never have a day or time off unless there is some way you can get someone to give you respite care.

I have a sister. When my parents were younger and in better health I would send them to her for several weeks every year, maybe twice to give myself a little break. This was beneficial from two points of view. One, it gave me a break and two, it helped her understand a little bit better what I was going through in trying to care for them. I would frequently talk to her on the phone to tell her how things were going with Mom and Dad, but she really, really didn't understand how difficult it was to take care of them until she had her turn to do it for a while. The last time she had Mom and Dad at her home for more than a few days it was so draining on her and so difficult that she got shingles. It usually comes out when you are under a lot of stress, and it's very painful. It takes a long time to get over it, you have to be on pain medication. Even with medication she was in excruciating pain for six weeks. But, that just gives you an idea of the stress it puts you under while caring for parents. Now, she has a much greater appreciation for what I have gone through. Still it is much different when you have them day in and day out, almost every day of the year.

Dad died six months ago, now I still have mother. A neighbor told me, "He was in his nineties. You ought to be happy he lived that long!"

An interesting thing my husband used to say, "I hope for your sake that your mother goes first because she is going to be a handful." To get along with the downside of her personality, Dad would roll with the punches. For everybody else to get along with her on a daily basis is a piece of work. I'm doing it all by myself. No one to share the burden. Whenever people find out that I'm taking care of my mother, most say, "That's nice that you can do that. Aren't you glad that you are able to do it?" They haven't a clue what the downside is. Or they will say, "Have you thought of putting her in a nursing home?" Well, yes, the thought has crossed my mind. I promised my parents years ago not to do that. Another reason is that I have never found a place that I would want a parent to be in. It is an option out there, it's not an option for me. I will keep my promise.

Most of the negative part is that there is no one in my life who really understands what it's like. Mothers of young children are the closest who could understand. Probably no one else really understands. I don't have a soulmate that I really can talk to about the trials I am going through.

The negative side is when people don't understand when you try to verbalize. It is very, very irritating on a daily basis if a parent is trying to tell you what to do. It sounds petty in the telling but as an adult you don't want somebody to tell you what to do unless you ask for advice. If you are asking for advice, fine. Otherwise you don't want somebody telling you what to do as if you were a child. So people who don't have their parents living with them or don't see them on a regular basis can't really relate to what it's like.

The hardest is dealing with my mother's moods. She can get into a bad mood and nothing is right. Everything is negative, she can't see anything positive or anything she can be grateful for. She complains about everything. It's hard to be around a person who is so negative and depressed all the time. Nothing you can do to make things different. If one could do or say something which would make things brightened up, feel good and have a good day. But it's incredibly difficult to be around someone who is negative all the time.

I can't stop and take the time to visit with someone. When we go to church, if I see someone after the service that I want to visit with, she is always there saying, "Lucy, I want to go *now*. Why can't we go *now*." If I say, " Mother, I want to visit with this person. We will leave in a little bit," a couple of seconds it's again, "Can't we go *now*? I want to go *now*." So, I can never enjoy a conversation with somebody when she is there with me. I always have to be concerned that she is waiting and doesn't want to wait. So the only time I can really enjoy time with friends or visit, I have to make special arrangements to have her taken care of. I just can't visit with friends when I want to. Any place we might go, it is always the same thing. That is very difficult because I am a social outgoing person and if I see someone I want to talk with I don't want to hear, "I want to go *now*." So many times I catch myself thinking, when I don't have that responsibility anymore I'll enjoy doing so and so and so. The list is growing longer. Things that I will again enjoy when I can do it again.

Feeling this way brings guilt feelings. You know that you would like to be able to do things without planning for your parent. But when you stop and think about it, on a day by day, by day basis, weeks and months and years you *can't* do what you want to do. This child of yours is not growing up and will never be able to be on their own. You can't leave and do what you want for periods of time. They are not going to their friend's house for an evening, overnight or weekend. Then you would be free to do anything you want if children are taken care of. That's not the situation with a parent.

Mother is a twenty-four hour responsibility. She only goes someplace if arrangements are made and it's more complex than hiring a babysitter. It's not something that goes away, in fact as she grows older the more difficult it gets. I need some time and space away, I need to be able to leave Mom at home and have her well taken care of, looked after. I need to feel the freedom of going out and doing something I enjoy doing once in a while. One day I called my brother because I needed help. His answer was to the point, "It's your thing to find someone."

Here the understanding from others comes into play. People could figure out another way of doing things, so they aren't inconveniencing me in order to get their needs met.

Dad had been diagnosed with Alzheimer's, a disease I never wanted to know anything about until I was faced with it. Over a period of several years, Dad's memory was getting worse. I was chalking it up to old age. It eventually got very bad. When I came home from work he would always ask, "How was your day?" I would tell him a little about my day's work. Say it was okay or go into more details. I would hardly finish before he would again ask the same question, "How was your day?" Exactly the same question not remembering that we had just talked about it. Sometimes it would happen time after time in the space of less than an hour.

His conversations became more limited to certain pat questions. It became very difficult to be patient. I was tempted to not even answer like I had not heard him. It's amazing how difficult it is to answer the same question over and over again, pretending it's the first time you heard the question. He had no memory for common occurrences. Things he had done for years seemed like he was doing them for the first time. Dad would say, "I've never done this before. Are you sure that's the way we are supposed to do it?" He would not remember if he'd had a bath or ate. When so much memory is lost, it was very draining, incredibly frustrating to be around him all the time and very oppressive. You just wanted to scream. One woman told me, "At least Alzheimer patients can walk!"

At the same time, I felt very bad for Dad. I couldn't relate or understand. The last six months of his life were an inconceivable nightmare. I was thankful for him that he didn't last a long time after he was very bad with the disease. At times, he would be very sad and cry, "I never wanted to be like this. When it was my time to go, I wanted to go quickly. I didn't want to be a burden to anyone." He worried that I was working too hard taking care of him. He wished he could just go to sleep. He was aware sometimes that his memory was really bad.

A week before he died he was unable to swallow. I couldn't successfully feed him, he would choke. I feared he would aspirate the soft food or fluids into his lungs. Dad had also told me that it would not be much longer. He seemed to know that the end was near. Because Dad had told me a long time ago that he didn't want any heroic measures, wanted to be a NO-CODE, he didn't have a feeding tube. Following his wish we let nature take its natural course. We kept him comfortable. With an eye dropper I kept his mouth and lips moist.

The hardest part is that people and friends don't understand. They don't know what to say, like there has been a death. But many others say the usual clichés:

How lucky they are to have you.
How lucky you are to have your parents so long.
What a wonderful person you must be.
How nice to have them home all the time.
I am sure this experience will bring your family closer.
You must be learning so much from this experience.
It's character building!

You know that there is no understanding behind what they are saying. I juggle the responsibilities of my job, a household and caring for my mother. There is a concert that I want to go to and I haven't been able to hire someone to stay with mother. It is very difficult to take her out in the evening. She doesn't want to go out. She wants to stay home. When it's dark outside she thinks its bedtime. I have a son and daughter, occasionally when I can't make any other arrangements I will ask them to help me. I was talking to my son about coming over to stay with her for an evening so I could go out. He told me, "Mom, Grandma would like to go to that. Don't you think she would like to do that?" "No, that's why I am asking you." I need some time to myself.

Who takes care of the caregivers?

Often when I show a little bit of abruptness because I am so tired, people tell me "Be patient." What do they think I do *all* day? My patience is pushed to the end.
Letter from a woman whose husband suffers from Alzheimer's.[1]

I could use a change of scenery. Newel and I are together so much. I am thankful he is most of the time, easy going. Lately, he is getting a little bit more stubborn, so unlike him. I attribute it to his forgetfulness. These days his decline is more apparent. Not a day goes by that I don't see an incident due to his illness. At times he reminds me of a little boy. He walks in the neighborhood. When he gets lost, someone will bring him home.

---

1 **Author's note:** Alzheimer's is a progressive brain disorder that produces loss of recent memory and reduces skills necessary for independent living. It effects over four million Americans and is the most devastating long term disease. It can last from five to six years.

"If we make our goal to live a life of compassion and unconditional love, then the world will indeed become a garden where all kinds of flowers can blossom and grow."

—*Elisabeth Kubler-Ross*

☏ Alzheimer's Association   (800) 272-3900
☏ Eldercare Locator: helps caregivers locate
   local services for the aging   (800) 677-1116

Publications

📖 *Caretakers, the Forgotten People*   (800) 848-1192
📖 "A Path for Caregivers" (D12957)
   AARP, 601 E St., NW, Washington, DC 20049

VOLUNTEERS

There was once a man vacationing on the coast. One evening he decided to take a midnight stroll down the deserted beach. There was a full moon so he could make out what appeared to be a boy who would scurry around, pick something up and throw it into the ocean.

As the man drew closer, he could see that the beach was littered with starfish. When he reached the boy, he asked him what he was doing. The boy explained that with each full moon the high tide would wash the starfish so far up the beach that they were destined to die the next day in the sun.

The man responded that there must be thousands of miles of beach and millions of stranded starfish. How much difference could this boy hope to make?

The boy looked back at the starfish in his hand, tossed it as hard as he could back into the life-saving sea and answered, "It made a difference to that one."

Remarks from people who meet a Hospice volunteer:
"Isn't it depressing?"
They would not do it if it was.

"You must be an angel!"

They are volunteers by choice, not by force of character.

In this jungle world of greed, looking out for *numero uno*, and getting-them-before-they-get-you mentality, volunteers are like an *oasis*.

There isn't anything in the world more uplifting than watching people help one another. Only volunteers are privileged to look into the eyes of that kind of human spirit. It is their reward.

"To know even one life has breathed easier because of you is to have succeeded."

—*Ralph Waldo Emerson*

"Caring can be learned by all human beings, can be worked into the design of life, meeting an individual need as well as pervasive need in society."

—*Composing Life, Mary Catherine Bateson*

Part 6

VIOLENCE

INCEST

Jill is a statuesque blonde with beautiful legs like Betty Grable. She is a paralegal secretary in a large San Francisco law firm.

It wasn't until I was twenty that I told a counselor, the very first person. It was weird. Even though I was not, it felt like I was lying. It was so difficult. The counselor expected the problem to be fixed in a couple of months, then I would feel better. He finally told me, "I don't know how to help you anymore." It was a gift, but at that time I felt that I was really, really sick and messed up if he gave up on me. It took me a long time to realize that he didn't have the skills. That's hard. I know other survivors who have gone through the same. I would have rather he had told me up front, "I don't know what to do with this issue" and referred me to someone else.

When I first went to Incest Survivors Anonymous, I looked at the floor the whole time. It was really, really hard. I was carrying a lot of my Dad and Mom's shame as well as my own. It took me almost two years before I could tell someone that I was an incest survivor and not feel bad about myself. I felt dirty, that it was all my fault. If I had been a better kid he would not have done it. It took me quite a while to realize that it was not my fault. Would people believe me? Most people said that they were sorry.

Basically it started when I was five. A couple things happened before that. The worst was from age nine until I was fourteen. To me, incest is the most selfish crime there is because they get their needs met, a kick out of what they are doing. They don't care about the effects of what they are doing on somebody else. It's true of every crime, but so much is stolen from a child. You lose your childhood. Perpetrators often say, "They were just a kid, they'll get over it. It's not that big a deal. It felt good anyway, didn't it?" They don't get how much damage they are doing and how long lasting the damages. They think you can go on and have a life.

I consider myself a survivor, and a thriver. I don't like to be called a victim anymore. It's hard to make people understand that the aftereffects are lifetime. People say, "It happened years ago, forget it."

Often people say, "Did it really happen? How can you remember for sure? Kids make up things all the time." The biggie is not being believed. Sometimes lack of belief is in things left unsaid.

There isn't always penetration, but for me there was for part of it. If there was not penetration, a father will say, "The only thing I did was touch her breast! That's no big deal!"

Some kids are told, "You are such a flirt. You should have known better than to walk around in your pajamas." Give me a break, she is only a kid. Parents are responsible for teaching them, but kids get blamed.

When mothers are confronted with the fact the usual response is, "My husband wouldn't do it! He is not that kind of a person. I don't know what's wrong with my daughter."

This is said when it is the husband, but when it is another family member or an outsider mothers are more likely to believe their daughters.

In my support group there is a gal who was sexually abused by her father with penetration for five years and the mother knew it. When confronted the mother's response was, "I prayed to God to fix it!" It was her place to make it stop.

So many people involve God, "God will take care of it." Or worse, "Just forgive him!" Church was important to me. I was told, "If you don't forgive him, you are *sinning*." I was sinning because I have not forgiven *him*! Forgive him! It *happened*! My goal was not to forgive but accept that indeed it happened, that he was sick and made poor choices. I don't take that responsibility away from him. He could have gone for help. I chose a different route by not shunning my parents. I didn't want to shut the relationship off.

Since then I have been working on my issues and after all these years, I look for what is good in him today. He has been sober for many years. My mother's behavior has changed. I split it between the dad who was wrong and the man who is here today.

Mothers do get blamed. There is a different kind of anger that I have had towards my mother than towards my father because she knew about it and didn't get me out of it. The fact is that she cared more about herself than getting me out of the situation. It's a lot harder to fathom how it affects you. Moms are supposed to be the nurturers and caretakers. That's the role they were given, the one they probably need to fulfill. That's the way God made it, men have certain gifts and women have others.

Typical clichés people say to me and other incest survivors, "It happened long ago, forget it! She enjoyed it anyway. It felt good, so it couldn't have done any harm." That's ridiculous. From boys I dated when they found out, "You got started early." Like telling me I shouldn't be upset about it. Male incest survivors hear these unkind words all the time. "What kind of training did you get? After all you just got an early start."

For a lot of incest survivors there is no proof. A minority of kids have physical damage as a result of it. Children are often asked the following question, "Are you sure it happened?" The child can't prove it. "Maybe it was a dream. You are heading towards puberty so maybe it's just a fantasy. Maybe you saw it in a movie, it wasn't really you." There are a lot of different things that will come up that way.

People in relationships, "I don't know if I want to take all that on." That's where that *stained* part takes place. Now you have a hideous feature they won't accept. It's very difficult in a relationship, it's hard to *trust*. We survivors, until we can trust, we need to be asked, "Is it okay to touch you, put my arms around you?" A lot of men don't want to deal with any repercussions.

Pain comes from people who make stupid remarks like, "You must have leaned too close to him while he was trying to watch TV. You cuddled too close to him. You sat on his lap too much. You kissed him, you touched him. You shouldn't have worn those short shorts in front of your Dad." The list is endless. Who is buying the kids' clothes? Some fathers will say, "I asked her, she said it was okay! She liked it. She is my little princess. We were just playing doctor. I was teaching her about sex." She sure should learn about sex other ways.

Another remark I heard a lot, "But he was an alcoholic, it wasn't his fault." I hate this one more than any other one. I hate it, to this day I still hate it. My mother to this day still says it. Nothing is his fault. BS, he is an adult. He is *responsible*. *He still made that choice*. My father made the choice of going through my bedroom door, at night alone, made the choice of getting into my bed.

We are still putting blame on the victims instead on the perpetrators. That's when the forgiveness comes in. It let's him off. Perpetrators have not been held accountable. Excuses anger me. "He had to do it, he had an urge. He had to do it because his wife was not available." It happens to some kids when their Mom is in the hospital. "Somebody had to meet that need!" These are *kids*, *kids*. Those needs can be checked, handled otherwise on one's own.

They are not going to die if they don't get their own sexual needs met. It's the dads who are the ones who should put a stop to this abuse, not the kids. It's not the kids' fault.

The idea of a child used as a sex object is abhorrent. It seems that these men feel that once the kids grow up, the memory, the damage will all go away. If kids are forced to watch pornography or perform sex, it will not go away at the end of their childhood. It will still be there.

Remember the film *The Exorcist*? What impact did playing that part have on the young actress? It's no wonder that she has problems today. All she was doing was acting a role. She didn't have to live that in her everyday life. But if you put a child through these things it is going to affect them. It does not wash off.

People in churches make the kids feel more guilty. Lots of blaming goes on.

The classics, "Why didn't you tell your Mom? Why didn't you tell your teacher? Why didn't you tell somebody? Why didn't you do something about it?" If you didn't do something about it, then it must not have happened, or must have been harmless. Can you imagine the fears that child has? Somehow children feel responsible. There is so much self-blame in sexual abuse. Also there's harm from keeping the shame hidden. Who will believe me? Some children are threatened. "Your Mommy is going to leave you if you tell" or "I'll hurt somebody if you tell." Kids believe that. They are little people. They can't see, that their father who threatens probably can't or won't carry out the threats.

Most common clichés, "Just get over it. Get on with your life. Don't continue dwelling on the past. Don't look back. Leave the past in the past." Those clichés pushed me to the point of exasperation.

They are kids, they are kids, *only* little kids.

Excruciating violation. Terrible injustice of being intimately harmed sexually by a parent. It may not leave visible bruises or broken bones, but injuries are profound and long lasting.

"Compassion is an alternate perception."

—*M.C. Richards*

☎ VOICES in Action, Inc. (Victims of Incest Can Emerge Survivors)   (312) 327-1500

RAPE

Pearl was born in a small Appalachian Mountain town where everyone was practically related to everyone else. She is a lively petite, white-haired woman with luminous greenish eyes. From the time she could walk, Pearl would constantly be in and out of her relatives houses. Now in her late seventies, she has been widowed for fifteen years.

When I was eighteen, one evening I went to my distant cousin Tim's house for supper. His sister and brother-in-law would also be there. After we ate, I was very tired as I had worked a long shift at a small factory. I asked Tim if I could lay down for a while. I left them watching TV and drinking beer. I kicked my shoes off and went to sleep, on the bed fully dressed.

Later I woke up with a start. Tim was on the bed tearing my clothes off. I struggled, tried to get away from him, scratching and kicking. I couldn't get away, and he wouldn't stop. I screamed hoping that his sister would hear me. He raped me, and raped me. Exhausted, I gave up. I was shocked, terrified. I kept my eyes tightly closed praying that it was only a nightmare. I was a virgin. He was rough, so the pain was unbearable. He even sodomized me. He finally got tired. Shaking all over, I walked painfully to the living room. His sister and brother-in-law were gone. I had planned on being a virgin when I got married — he took that away from me.

Tim followed me and sat next to me. He said, "Oh! What did I do to you? I did it because I wanted you so."

I was in shock. He wanted to make me a cup of tea. I only wanted to take a shower and get out of there as soon as possible. I wanted to leave, get away, didn't want him near me. I couldn't talk, wished he was dead.

I started to put my clothes on. He wouldn't let me go. He dragged me back to the bedroom, and kept raping me. He finally fell asleep from exhaustion. I grabbed my clothes, silently dressed in the living room. I walked out and down the screechy porch steps, terrified that he would hear me. I went to a friend's house, a nurse. As soon as I walked in she said, "What's wrong with your clothes?" Sobbing, I answered, "I was raped." Her next comment was unbelievable, "You must have encouraged him somehow. How did it feel?"

Blindly, I left, not having recollections of how I got home. It was the end of our friendship.

I didn't tell anyone else. I was so ashamed, embarrassed, and felt like scum. I thought that everyone could see that I had been raped. They would think that I was a horrible person. I didn't know if anyone would believe me because everyone knew Tim.

The following day I went to see the doctor who asked me, "How did he do it?"

Not understanding I questioned him, "What do you mean?"

"Was he gentle?"

"Gentle! How can it be? I was raped! Violent rape."

The doctor finally said, "I am sorry." I didn't get any support from him.

I didn't see Tim for a couple of weeks because I avoided him. I was staying at my aunt's house. When he started coming over, I wouldn't answer the door. One day Auntie said that he wanted to talk to me. Tim had come to ask if I wanted to go the Smith's party. I told him that I had been invited and would go alone.

At the party Tim got drunk. During the evening, standing not far away, I heard him say to a friend, "I got Pearl. I scored, went all the way. Pay on the bet."

His friend answered, "Way to go!"

Tim was bragging. His friend paid him, I saw it. I was so revolted, I left the party. I couldn't believe that someone could ruin my life to win a bet. He *knew* that I was a virgin. Tim wanted to win the bet, that's all there was to it.

Years later a woman told me, "When men rape, it's because they just can't control themselves!" Really! Are they animals?

I went back to the doctor because I thought I was pregnant. He asked me if I was going to have an abortion stating, "After all, it was rape. You'll be better off."

I finally told my aunt that I was pregnant. She knew something was wrong. She hugged me, but didn't know what to say or do. Auntie asked me if I was going to keep the baby. I said, yes. Still she always implied that it was my fault, that I shouldn't have gone to Tim's. She kept adding that he was a *nice* guy.

One day while Auntie had gone to a church meeting, Uncle Joe, her husband and I were having a cup of coffee. As I was leaving, I bent down to kiss him on the cheek like I always did. He grabbed me and kissed me on the mouth. Laughingly, he explained his behavior by saying, "Tim scored, he went all the way. You have a bun in the oven." His thinking was after all I was pregnant, unmarried so he could do anything he wanted to do. I told Auntie. She didn't believe me, called me a liar. "You know your uncle. He is a hugger."

I couldn't believe all these things happening to me. When I was with friends, I heard remarks. People laughing behind my back,

"Here goes the virgin! She is pregnant and not married. Poor thing!"

One of Tim's friends told me, "Why don't you leave him, come with me. I'll show you a good time."

Living in a small town made it worse. Everyone knew Tim. He had a bad reputation except with Auntie. She wouldn't admit that I had been raped. She kept on saying, "You must have encouraged him somehow. You slept in his bedroom. You didn't fight hard enough. You really could have gotten away. After all he was drunk." She would go on and on.

Another remark was totally the opposite, "Why didn't you just submit? He wouldn't have been so violent!"

Tim one day came over. He told Auntie that he wanted to take care of the baby.

After he left she came to my room. "Better marry him," she said. "No one else will marry you. He is a nice guy, has a good heart." Again she added, "After all that day he was drunk." Against my better judgement, I married him. What was I to do? In that small town there was no chance to get away. How would I support myself and the baby?

My mother who lived in a small village fifty miles away came over. She said that she was sorry and that there was nothing she could do. When Mom got home, she told the rest of the family, my brothers and sister the story of my rape. When I saw my family, one brother made the remark, "How does it feel to be part of the *in* crowd? If it is a boy, he'll grow up to be like his father — no good. You'll bring another rapist into the world."

My sister said, "You are in the ranks of women who had sex before marriage. You fell! You are finally human." She thought it was great that I was pregnant.

A friend told me, "Why did you stay out so late? Why were you wearing that short skirt?"

My older brother petted my belly, grinning he said, "I am going to be an uncle! I am glad you didn't stay a virgin until you got married." How disgusting!

When I saw my father he treated me like garbage which is surprising as he was no angel. He told me the old cliché, "You made your bed, you lie in it! It was really your fault. You slept at his house. He was drunk. You are making a big deal of it. Women get raped all the time and go on with their lives." Women are always blamed, especially in those days.

I stayed away from my friends, humiliated, afraid of their scorn and remarks. On Sundays when I went to church, remarks were constantly made. Even some young men after church, smirking and whispering, "Want to go to bed?"

I went from a virgin to supposedly a *prostitute*.

Nothing was said about him! For him it was a great deal, macho... After all he was *drunk*! Excuses...Excuses...Same excuse.

Rape is like surgery. It hurts terribly, plus inflicting total humiliation and shame. The only thing Tim was attracted to was my *body*, nothing else. He had bragged that he could have any woman he wanted. Men's egos push them to prove that they can have any woman they want. SO WHAT? What's the big deal? You want 100 of them — have them, but leave the virgins alone. Tim's friends knew that given the chance, Tim would sleep with or rape anyone with skirts.

After my cute little girl was born, Tim came to the hospital to pick me up. From that day on he never drank again. He had raped me during the pregnancy, my baby was born prematurely.

After we were married Tim started to say to anyone who would listen,

"She is *mine*!" Sometimes he grabbed my breast in public, "Those are *mine*." He would tell me, "You married me, you signed papers. You are *mine*."

It was years before I realized that marriage licenses don't have the word *possession* or *ownership* anywhere in them.[1]

"The world is a dangerous place, not because of those who do evil, but because of those who look on and do nothing."

—*Albert Einstein*

☎ Against Our Will   (518) 434-0439
(peer support group for sexual assault survivors)

---

1   **Author's note:** She is *mine* claims ownership. That woman is paid for. Owning means slavery. XIII section 1, December 18, 1865. Twenty-seven states out of thirty ratified XIII amendment. "Neither slavery nor involuntary servitude except as punishment for crime duly convicted, shall exist within the United States…"

   Victims of rape feel that the attack has made them worthless and that others will think so too. The outrage, the self-blame, and finally the psychological numbness are like going through a dark tunnel. On the other side life is *never* going to be the same again.

   Rape is a crime that uses sex to express rage and violence. We should shame entertainment companies that traffic in rap-music lyrics that *glorify* rape.

   It is estimated that in the United States 20 percent of women are raped, 280 women a day.

DOMESTIC VIOLENCE

Norma has a smooth olive complexion, dark brown eyes, and lush black hair combed in a bouncy pageboy style.

Society is very critical of battered women. Why not the men who inflict the abuse? Women are told to get help, let's start with the batterers.

People need to eliminate many clichés from their vocabulary about domestic violence. Their reactions are horrendous!

"Why does she stay?"

There is an illusion that she can leave! He can follow her in many ways.

"She asked for it! She must have done something to make him mad."

Abused women want to be believed when they say, "He is going to kill me."

Engage Brain Before Speaking

· I didn't tell anyone about the violence in my marriage. I was scared. I kept it to myself. I didn't even tell my family.

Several years after we got married, Sam hit me with a wine bottle on the nose. It was hard to deal with. I stayed inside as much as I could, too embarrassed to go out. When I did I lied about the cut on the bridge of my nose, giving the excuse that I had banged myself in the dark against a door.

Sam was always nice to everybody, the good *old boy*.

It was *my* life, it was not a big deal to me. Anyhow his abuse started out very slowly and gradually. I'm asked, "How did you live through all that?" You did it, that was it. That's all I knew. I grew up knowing that. My first memory is of my father knocking my mother out of a chair.

People's reactions to Sam's abuse were horrible. They drown me with their empty reactions, "Oh! My God. How did you live with that? How did you deal with that?"

I would think, "What's the big deal?" But deep down I was immobilized by fear, unable to act. Constant anticipation of abuse.[1]

If I had not lied about all the times Sam hit me everyone would have found out. It was not something that happened all the time. During our ten years of marriage,

---

1   **Author's note:** Women don't choose to live with a violent partner, but have chosen to continue living with someone they've learned to love. Most batterers abuse their wives/partners *after* a strong emotional relationship has developed.

he only hit me four or five times a year . But those times were bad enough. The rest of the time he was good. Some women say it happens to them all the time. But, with Sam you never knew when it would happen. That's what keeps you on pins and needles. Scared all the time, never knowing what would set him off. It is called *walking on eggs*. That is what I had seen when I grew up, and thought was normal. The world revolved around Sam's selfish ways and he was always abusive about it. If he didn't get what he wanted, tamper tantrums and abuse would follow easily and violently. He lived in two gears, blowing up and making love.

I got to the point that I didn't care what people thought or said. I was who I was.

Why don't abused women leave the men who batter them?[1] Why don't they run away? There are no easy answers. To name a few, hope he will change, denial — shame — fear of worse, death. The fear is real considering the violence perpetrated against women who have left their abusers. How many have died?

When people say about women in abusive relationships, "Why doesn't she leave?" They don't know any-

---

1   Author's note: Abuse is often not reported due to fear of revenge. Leaving often means a death sentence. Considering the options, it often takes a great amount of courage to leave. Most of these women have no means of support. Some may become homeless to escape the danger. During the year 1996, in Arizona 27,000 were turned away from shelters for lack of room. What options do these battered women have?

thing about domestic violence. But, surprisingly I have found myself doing the same thing. Women don't support each other.

"Why doesn't she get out." Part of me knows why, knows how it is.

SHE ASKED FOR IT.

What a *stupid, stupid* thing to say. *Nobody asks for it.* She doesn't know how to make her needs known or what she wants. Her partner does not either or he would not do it the way he does. Victims end up having to defend themselves.

It is something a man learns, that it is okay to hit a woman to get what he wants. To control her with violence. Batterers use their inebriation as an excuse for their violence. Batterers need to be taught that things can be different, to learn, and have the will to change. THERE IS NO EXCUSE FOR DOMESTIC VIOLENCE.[1]

When Sam told me, "You make me angry," he had a choice whether to control that anger. He would not hit me in front of other people, always behind closed doors. It shows that he could control his anger.

Batterers can always find an excuse for their violence. (dinner is not on time, the house is dirty, she is getting fat). The list is endless. If his wife/companion/lover has a boyfriend, *STILL* there is no *EXCUSE* to kill her. Instead why don't we ask, *"WHY DOESN'T HE*

---

[1] Author's note: Solving domestic violence is also men's work. Men need to tell batterers that their behavior is not acceptable. They need to speak out against domestic violence.

LEAVE? Get rid of her, get a divorce. That man has all kinds of options. Better he talk to her about what she wants to do. But, NO his ego was hurt. Sam couldn't stand the thought that he didn't have complete control over me.[1]

They batter because they CAN. Because it WORKS and because NOBODY stops them.

People said Sam is such a *nice guy*. Most batterers are nice guys, that's why women stay with them, but for some 20 percent of the time they are not. That's what keeps her there, 80 percent is good, 20 percent bad. We keep *hoping* the situation is going to change because our men promise it will never happen again. They profess their love. The 80 percent guy is fun to be with, once in a while his behavior is too much. We often survive on HOPE. Always promised he would never do it again. "Lost my head. I love you. I'll never do it again." Apologies are addictive. We are also immobilized and unable to act.

I so often prayed to God, I would not leave, would stay with this man for the rest of my life, but don't let him hit me. I felt trapped like an hostage. He had all the power. I felt chained to him in my head. With hostages we send

---

[1] **Author's note:** It is a myth that men can't control their anger. If they were offered a large monetary reward, would they continue? Rarely. If someone would ring the doorbell, would they continue in front of a visitor? Domestic abuse is done behind closed doors in the confines of a home. Most batterers have poor skills for coping with stress, but they know very well what they are doing.

help. With women, they are called *crazy bitches* otherwise they would walk out.

One week-end he lifted his fist and threatened our son. Then waved a gun taken out of his pocket, screaming, "I am going to kill you all." Our boy started whimpering. *That was it!* I didn't want that man to hurt my son, anymore than he had been. I screamed, "Don't touch him, don't you *ever, ever* touch him."

For a lot of women that's what does it. We have to get to a point that we want better than that. The fear for my son's life did more than anything else to get me to leave. I was not going to let my son go through that kind of threats for the rest of his life. At that time he was seven. Sam was arrested then released. I got an order of protection. He took it as revoking his power to *control* me by means of a marriage contract.

Three weeks later before sunrise, he opened the door of my apartment with his key. At that time I didn't know he had been released, and hadn't had the locks changed. Sam walked right in, pulled me out of the bed, beat me up and *stabbed* me in the throat. I have a long scar from under the side of my chin to my collar bone. I was hospitalized for a week. My Mom took care of my son. I was attacked in my home, which should have been a safe place for me and my son.

He was sentenced to fifteen years in the state prison.[1]

---

1 Author's note: In sentencing, battering should be treated like any other aggravated assault case. Especially NO parole.

That's the last time I saw Sam.

That attack was a wake-up call that I will never forget which has left long term aftereffects. He had *allowed* his anger to control him. During those years I knew that men can control their rage more than they care to admit. Sam always had excuses for the violence, "That's the way I am!" That's NEVER a valid excuse. When he drank, he was the one who brought the glass to his lips. No one forced him. Even in public, verbal batterers *choose* their time and place. I pity him that he will never have a life that's any different than it was. But I still get overwhelmed with fear. Statistically, my ex-husband is a lost cause. It is sad. He has two children from a previous marriage that he never sees. I was married to Sam for ten years, and I never met them.

I'd rather be alone forever rather than living the way we did. I know that I am worth more than the life I had. There is something else better out there for me.

Domestic violence in general has nothing to do with the welfare system. Batterers think, "I can hit, I can control, and I can do what I want." That's not true. People need to be taught right from wrong. Until you change the way people think and the way they feel about themselves they are not going to change. There is so much work to do.

Callously and stupidly too many people say, "She must like it! Or she'd leave." Baloney! Those people don't know anything about domestic violence. If they did, they'd bury those thoughts. Our society in general has *no* compassion for what someone else is going through especially domestic violence.

I had left Sam many times. Like most batterers, every time I left he assumed that there was somebody else. He had low self-esteem and insecurities. Always, there could never be any other reasons. There never was anyone. He was not working. He was hitting me. It is a life I didn't want, but here I was in it. How do I get out of that? How do I change that? I didn't know how. Women who were in domestic violence relationships say, "If I had known..."

One time my sister said, "I don't know why you leave, you always go back." But that sister is also living in a violent marriage. She has never left. She spends weekends away sometimes, comes to my house. At times I need to go and get her. I will always have a place for her if she wants to leave.

A cousin made a remark about my situation, "Oh, well! It runs in the family."

I had to learn how to live my life and to be different, to look back at what was going on in my life. I had to do some real soul searching. We were two people, playing the game. A dance together, but if one partner does not do the same steps, things are not going to go right, things are going to change. I would leave the dance and it would not feel right. I was scared. I didn't want to end it as yet, didn't want to give up. I had bruises, black eyes and a broken nose. People didn't know because I lied. Maybe they did and didn't say anything. I never showed any feelings because I didn't know how. Everything was stifled. At our house, when we were young, we were not allowed to cry, not allowed to get mad. So we learned to bottle all that up.

I can remember the first time I ever got angry, allowing myself to feel. I had all those feelings in my body and didn't know what they were. First time I felt anything I got flushed in the face. It was so overwhelming that I was scared to death. It took a lot of therapy, a lot of willingness to change. I am not done with me by a long shot, I have a lot of work yet to do. When I am done, I'll be dead. I can wait. Living is a process of trial and error. Domestic violence is a big part of my life, all of my life. Change takes a lot of inner searching. Willingness to admit that I had a part in this relationship, the part of the victim. A part I had learned all my life. You have to be willing to look at that and if you are not, you are not going to change a lot.

There is no meaning to life when you are married in name only to an abusive husband. Life is split in half, but there is no sharing. Only constant taking without regard to what truly matters.

I was asked, "What are you willing to do to change your life?"

Right then, I was willing to do whatever I needed to do. It was a beginning. I decided to change. It's hard to understand in our hearts that we need to learn the real work of healing. I had a hard time meeting people. I had to learn to think for myself, accept myself the way I was. When people don't know anything about domestic violence, why bother listening to them? But deep down, people's comments hurt. So many times their careless remarks reinforced my low self-esteem, that I was worthless, and the stupidest woman in the world. Nobody could ever be as low as I was. Why would anybody put themselves through this? Every abused woman believes she is alone. That nobody else could understand what she is going through.

First time I left, oh, God! I was petrified. I went to my sister's, then my parents'. My mother never reproached me.

I didn't contact the clergy because we were not a church-going family. But I know that some clergy tell women that their place is staying with their husbands. Keep the family together for the children's sake, often telling them, "Be a better wife." Putting the responsibility of the marriage on women's shoulders. What do they tell the batterers? Did anyone ever tell them to be better husbands? Never.

Probably these clergymen have never experienced someone beating the hell out of them. I don't think God meant to have women battered, or meant to have anyone live like that.

When I talk about my ex-husband my parents say that their pain watching me was worse than mine. Our pain is worse than yours. It is a very selfish attitude.

Every person's pain is their own pain. Maybe what happened to me is not the worst that can happen to someone, but it's *was my pain*, not anyone else's.

During my marriage I was rarely verbally abused. Sam never called me names. It was his *fists* that I was afraid of. What could I do to make him keep them in his pockets?

My father was verbally abusive. Whenever we dated, Dad called us whores, bitches out for only one thing. We were supposed to be in by eleven. One evening, my older

184

sister was out with her steady boyfriend. My mother told Dad, "She is fifteen minutes late."

He answered, "It's only takes fifteen minutes." At that time I was very naive and was very disappointed that whatever it was took only fifteen minutes.

Sam was the first man I ever dated and I was infatuated so fast. I knew absolutely nothing about men. I learned TOO quick. I can't say that Sam was bad all the time. When he was good, he was the kindest man. If you never saw him drunk and violent, you would have never believed his bad side. Kids loved him and that's how I used to judge people. If kids liked somebody, they couldn't be all bad. He was a man who didn't know how to use, or what to do, with his feelings. He didn't realize that he didn't have to control me, didn't have to tell me what to do. Most of the time he didn't apologize, he didn't have to. I was there anyway. Still violence was *his* choice.

I would like a man in my life, but I don't trust. If I do I am afraid I might go overboard. I am very open, and willing to share.

I have been divorced for seven years. I've been bringing up my son alone.

Soon, Sam is supposed to appear in front of the parole board. These are scary times.

I have met a woman who was shot by her husband. He had flown from the east coast to kill her. Very well planned and premeditated attempted murder.

Education needs to be started in kindergarten. Children need to learn — RESPECT others, from children to older people. Teach that arguments aren't solved by hitting. Speak out against bullies. High school girls need to be taught the *danger* signals of boyfriends' possessiveness and control. Isolation and spare time exclusively spent with a boyfriend aren't signs of a healthy relationship. Nor is a relationship where the boyfriend won't let her dance or talk with other boys.)[1]

No matter what the spouse does or fails to do in her abuser's eyes, she isn't the cause of the abuse. Her change of behavior will not stop the abuse.

Abusers are good at presenting an image of stability, responsibleness and sincerity. However at home they continue to be abusive. He is the *only* one in control of his violence. It's deliberate and focused on an intended victim — his *mate*.

Power and control is redefining the other person's view of themselves, redefining their beliefs.

It is estimated that in the United States, four million women are battered every year. An average of four women will die daily as the results of injuries. 95 percent of domestic violence attacks are committed by men against women. In 1994, among all female homicide victims, 27 percent were killed by a spouse or boyfriend. 3 percent of male victims were killed by a wife or girlfriend. (Federal Bureau of Investigation 1995)

In the U.S. we have three times more animals shelters than shelters for women and children.

---

1   Author's note: Some plays and movies glorify obsessive love giving the wrong message: *Phantom of the Opera*, obsessive love. *My Fair Lady*, a man shaping a young woman to fit his ideal.

"Let there be spaces in your togetherness, and let the winds of heaven dance between you. Love one another, but make not a bond of love."

—*The Prophet, Kahlil Gibran*

☎ National Coalition Against
   Domestic Violence   (303) 839-1852
☎ DOMESTIC VIOLENCE   (800) 333-7230
☎ TDD   (800) 787-3224
☎ Family Violence Prevention
   Fund Tel   (800) 313-1310

ELDER ABUSE

While visiting in a southeastern state, I interviewed the director of the Area on Aging.

Most of the elderly are competent and clear minded, capable of making sound decisions. The overly used cliché, *they are old*, they don't know what they are saying, they are crazy, senile are excuses to take advantage of them.

What are the types of elder abuse? When does it happen most often? Why does it occur?

Elder abuse consists of psychological, physical and financial abuse.

Psychological abuse is demeaning name calling or insults, "You are getting older, you don't remember." Threats of being taken to a nursing home. Ignoring elders, not taking them to the doctor, overlooking their complaints. Their self-esteem is severely abused.

Physical abuse, slapping, physical restraining, withdrawal of food or lack of proper food, not dispensing needed medications.

Financial abuse: fraud, illegally using funds in the form of cash or credit cards. Telemarketing fraud; mail and phone scams, charging for goods or services not delivered.

They are invisible victims. The abuse rarely comes to the attention of the criminal justice system. The elderly often have no means or ability to complain. If they do, caregivers say that they are senile.

Our society is a throw-away society. We care little about our elderly. Four out of five should be institution-alized, many institutions are crowded and some poorly run. Their caregivers want to keep them at home. Twenty per cent are taken care of by spouses, children, friends, neighbors or other unpaid caregivers.

Most elderly are not afraid to die, but of what happens when they get seriously ill.

Many have not made provisions like, "Who is going to make decisions if I have dementia?" Living trusts are very important as well as medical power of attorney.

We have older parents who help adult children who have drug or alcohol problems, afraid they might end up in the streets.

A man called me from the Midwest because his father was practically out of funds having made large withdraw-als. He didn't know what to do, what the problem was or how to solve it.

His mid-eighties father had met this cute little woman around sixty who told him,

"Trust me! I will take care of you."

They had a relationship that lasted about six months. She moved in to take care of him, do the shopping, and pay his bills. He would sign the checks, she then would insert the amount. In six months, she went through his entire savings and disappeared.

Older people are being exploited, victims of elder abuse, but not according to the law. This man wasn't legally incompetent, but was vulnerable. His son said that the only recourse was to hire an attorney because obviously there had been deception. It was a civil matter. The son added, "My father is a very proud man who will not go to court, stand up and say, 'I was a fool! I was fooled by this woman.'"

A seventy-seven-year-old woman, a retired RN, had raised three children. Her husband became seriously ill. "I'll take care of him," she said and refused help. At her age she was trying to provide twenty-four hour care. This type of issue is ignored by everyone.

What about older men trying to take care of their wives? For centuries women were responsible for the household and children. A man who has never changed a diaper, never given baths to his children, never prepared meals, now tries to take care for an ailing wife. He is doing the best he can. Our society has parenting classes, but no resources to teach a man how to take care of a patient and a household. Neither is education available for people called the *sandwich generation* who are trying to care for their aging parents directly, or worse, from out of town. It's a new phenomenon. A real caregivers' issue.

Other older abused women are being harmed by adult children or other family members. In the children instances, Is it a pay back?

"How sharper than a serpent's tooth it is to have a thankless child."

—*King Lear, Shakespeare*

Abusers isolate the victims first from family members, neighbors and friends.

In our state, abuse is defined as neglect, exploitation of a vulnerable or incapacitated adult. Most substantiated reports are neglect. But what to do when the perpetrator is self? Self neglect, refusing outside help. Elderly in reasonable good health who live alone, but don't take care of themselves, don't take baths, have a poor diet. A raging debate continues. People say, "You can't put self-neglect in the classification of elder abuse." The perpetrator and the victim are one and the same. Unfortunately, who is going to respond to that problem if there is not a state agency?

Another area that has been too long overlooked is older battered women. Especially the way they were socialized in the early twenties. You are married and hate your spouse and they may hate you, but you took those vows. Separation or divorce can't be imagined. You might kill the person or be killed but you are not going to divorce them. We had an eighty-three-year-old woman who was murdered by her husband of ninety. Here we have *traditions*. A survey of what was available for older battered women reveals there is *nothing*.

Many older women were raised to believe that family matters are private, not to be discussed with anyone, especially counselors, believing they don't need outside help. Generational, cultural and religious values have an impact on their decision to stay or leave. To leave would be failing at their most significant achievement.

Most older abused women are dependent on their abuser for financial support and fear ending in a nursing home, fear they'd have not enough income to live alone and maybe end up homeless. If the abuser is ill, pressure comes from family, friends and professionals to stay with him. One particular woman stayed, she felt obligated to care for her invalid husband who kept on abusing her verbally.

We had another case where the husband wouldn't pay for his wife's medication. His excuse was that she really didn't need it and it was much too expensive. While she was in the hospital, he didn't visit her.

HEALTH INSURANCE is of the most importance and a concern as most elderly women are covered by their husband's policy. Leaving might end coverage, and also result in poverty. Some older women have a lifetime of shared financial assets, but with no access to them. Some have jobs near retirement age, but still have no or limited retirement benefits. Others who want to enter the job market face age discrimination. Complicating the situation is *real* fear of living alone at her age. Additional barriers for leaving; loss of home and/or transportation.

In one domestic violence case, a woman had insisted on leaving the house to go to the movies with a new girlfriend she had met in the retirement area where the couple had moved in. Her husband started yelling at her, but she continued getting ready. He grabbed her arm and pulled her down the stairs. This was the first time he had been abusive to her. When he was asked why, he replied, "She had never *defied* me before."

Although the complexity of elder abuse can't be denied, people want a quick fix. When you have a dysfunctional family of fifty years, are you going to solve the problem in one week? Two weeks? A month or a year? It will take years or more likely may never be solved. Because of the way laws are written, our community is incapacitated and not geared to help older battered women. Most often these women are *not* incapacitated, nor incompetent. Each is a *victim* who is in need of services.

A number of factors account for older women not using domestic violence shelters. Domestic violence shelters are geared to younger women with children who need transitional housing. In most shelters, the woman has to be employed or in school. What can she do if she is in her eighties? Most shelters are filled with young families. Support group discussions are about child custody, day care, jobs, etc. SO, older women have had nowhere to turn for services.

Our agency received a call from a counselor who had a client angry to the point of hysteria. The woman was eighty, married at twenty, with the same man for sixty years. She finally said to herself, "I am not going to take it anymore." What help was available to her?

Her needs should be addressed. What must the system do? First, understand the victims. We *think* we know what their needs are.

Second, look at the legal services, divorce. He is the abuser, why should she have leave her house? Why is it that the victim is punished for the abuser's actions? Why is it that the victim has to go to a shelter? If you are accustomed to your own bed and room, how are you going to sleep in a bunk bed? Many of these women have additional basic needs. Shelters don't have nursing staffs, are not licensed to dispense medication. They are not equipped to help these older women. It is a very complex issue. She needs to have her self-esteem restored and to be built back to a whole person.

Why did she take the abuse so long? The question goes back to blaming the victim for the problem. Perhaps she needed long term health care. How is she going to get it if they separate? If she's a woman who stayed home, she won't have enough Social Security to live on. If she leaves, what is out there for her. Is there housing? Medical care? There's more than a two to three year wait for Section 8 housing assistance (rent subsidies). Where does she go in the meantime? We are looking at three or four issues. We can't just tell her to leave without having alternatives for her. Abuse is very slow and insidious. First the abuser gains the victims' trust, followed with isolation which is part of the control, which is then followed by degradation.

We also see abuse with caregivers' stress. Sickness can alter the healthiest of relationships. They have no relief, for example a spouse with dementia follows the caregiver eighteen hours a day asking the same questions. After many weeks the emotionally exasperated response may be, "I wish you were not here, I wish you were dead." Frustration can escalate to outbursts of anger pushed to desperation. My mother took care of my grandfather for one year, she aged twenty years during that time of twenty-four-hour care.

In 1994, 818,000 elderly were victims of various types of domestic abuse, and these are the ones which were reported! Often the elderly person is embarrassed or unable or afraid to report the abuse.

National estimated statistics from that state Area on Aging: 1.5 million cases annually of elder abuse. One in fourteen cases reported. Mostly women in their eighties.

"We realize that what we are accomplishing is a drop in the ocean. But if this drop were not in the ocean, it would be missed."

—*Mother Teresa*

"Independence? That's middle class blasphemy. We are all dependent on one another, every soul of us on earth."

—*George Bernard Shaw*

☎ National Center for Elder Abuse   (202) 682-0100
☎ Children of Aging Parents   (800) 227-7294
☎ AARP Consumers Affairs
   601 E St., NW
   Washington, DC 20049   (202) 434-2277
☎ National Fraud Information
   Center   (800) 876-7060
☎ National Senior Citizens
   Law Center   (202) 887-5280

MURDER

Susan is a pretty brunette in her late thirties. She is a very successful business woman. She has three children, one still living with her.

One evening, my daughter Marge's roommate Ruth called. She was concerned because she hadn't seen Marge for several days. Marge always told her roommate Ruth when she planned to stay somewhere overnight. I felt something was wrong. Someone always knew where Marge was. Without telling me Ruth had already turned in a missing person's report.

Two days later, a Saturday, the door bell rang. Two men were at the door.

They showed their badges, detectives. They told me that Marge's body had been found in the woods five miles out of town. Instant shock! Disbelief! Thank God Ruth had the wisdom not to tell me over the phone. The police had called her before the detectives came with the horrible news. This is how I found out that my nineteen-year-old daughter had been murdered.

At first people tried to make me believe they cared. They asked lots of questions. They wanted to know how she was killed, where she was found. Did they have a suspect? Was it someone she knew? Why? Why? Why all those questions? Questions, Questions!! Morbid curiosity?

One woman called. She had read the article on the murder in our local paper, recognized Marge's name. "Oh! Lord, don't tell me it's your daughter!" She sounded so compassionate. "Do call me sometime," she added. I don't recall if she was at the funeral or sent a card, but she never called me. It was strictly curiosity, an element of gossip.

The murder involved a small amount of drugs. Word got around because there were a few people in the house when the detectives came. Everyone had heard them. Someone with a big mouth left the house. That started some vicious rumors. It wasn't something I wanted a lot of people to know. We are a middle class family. I was embarrassed. My daughter was a wonderful, respectable girl. But, she just blew it. With all that vicious talk, was I supposed to conclude that Marge deserved to be shot?

In order to stop people from spreading more rumors, I had to avoid speaking about it. If I spoke about my feelings, it only fueled more questions. My cop-out was just to say, "I am not privileged to share additional information, police orders." Then I realized that people were talking behind my back. That hurt more than anything else. So I had to work through it alone.

A woman did something very cruel. She called the mother of my other daughter's fiance to tell whatever she knew. Susan's daughter has been murdered, the family is trash. Her malicious gossip came back to me. To think that a person would say such mean and hurtful things. Jack's mother was terribly upset, thinking that her son would also be murdered just because he was dating my other daughter. It was the most hurtful thing that anyone did because it was done intentionally. It caused quite a few problems between my daughter and Jack.

Because I am a single parent, of course people said, "Marge comes from a broken home. Look what happens to children whose parents are divorced."

I had to make new friends. There is only one of my old friends who is willing to listen to me. A few weeks later, I met a friend in the grocery store. She went on and on how she had fallen on the tennis court and broken her elbow. I felt like my insides had been pulverized. A little bit of the shock was starting to wear off and I am listening to her about her elbow. The conversation switched to Marge. This friend told me that IT WOULD BE WORSE for her because she only had one child. Now that I look back, I should have been impolite and said, *you are crazy*. Instead I politely listened until I was ready to throw up. I finally did tell her that each one of my children is *unique*. My grief is not lessened because I have other children. I found it easier to nod my head and almost give her, yes, yes, you must be right. I heard the same comment from many people, "At least, you have your other children." It's so insensitive. I was often admonished by, "You *must* be strong for them." I didn't want anyone telling me that I had to be strong, because I *couldn't* be.

Another person said, "You should be happy, Marge is in heaven." Even though that's true, because of my Christian beliefs, it doesn't erase the fact that physically speaking, she is dead and my heart is ripped out of my body.

It made me think that we live in a society where everything is instant, fix it up or patch it up. We are so used to trying to cheer people up and get them out of sad or horrendous situations. During conversations, to avoid their own discomfort, a lot of people changed the subject talking about something happy, thinking it would help me.

About a month ago I was telling a friend that I was depressed because of the holidays coming soon. The conversation was brief. She went on to tell me that death and divorce were the same thing! I was overwhelmed. I told her, "You don't understand. You are discounting my feelings." She promptly retorted, "No, I am not. I know. I just read it."

It started an argument, needless to say I haven't spoken to her again. She never called to apologize. I thought that she was a concerned, caring friend. Her comments lacerated my heart. By her authority, tone of voice, those few words revealed her hatefulness. It is true that my grief and suffering separates me from the rest of the world.

Three months after Marge's death I told a co-worker that I was having a bad day. She answered, "Really, what's wrong?" It crushed me. Another said that I should be *thankful* that I had nineteen years with my daughter. It would be worse if she was younger. WHY? It stabbed my heart.

People disappeared. This whole nightmare has made me reassess friendships, especially with people that I had on too high a pedestal. Not that I want to be reclusive about it, but I am very disappointed in mankind as a whole, very much so. To think that when you are down and out, the funeral is all over, they are gone. Very, very few of them even called to say, "How are you doing?"

When I reached the year mark people expected me to be *over it*. I should be *getting on*. When I had a bad day, they didn't want to hear about it any longer.

At the end of the trial the man who murdered Marge was found guilty. The verdict didn't make me feel better. Even after the way my daughter died, revenge was not the answer. It's up to the courts. I am still constantly asked, "How do you feel about it?" I refuse to answer.

Last week I went to a funeral which was my first since Marge died. It raked my soul. A woman from our church choir was there. She came over, took me in her arms and said, "I've heard that you had a hard time. I was thinking about you all week." I didn't even know that she knew me. Someone must have told her that it was the first anniversary of Marge's death. I just answered, "Thank you very much." Just knowing that she acknowledged my feelings, when my own friends wouldn't even discuss it. It helped tremendously.

What amazes me is now that the healing is starting to occur, I realize that I am stronger than those people.

Years ago I remember saying that it was just as well a beautiful young woman we knew was retarded because of teen drug and sex, she wouldn't be touched by any of it. My ex-husband had exclaimed, "How can you say that?" Now I realize that I had made a darn, stupid statement! I was trying to look at the bright side. That's why people say all this stuff. Many times there isn't a bright side. There isn't any silver lining when it comes to murder.

I have been hurt by WORDS and the lack of them. I am unable to mention Marge's name. It reinforces my knowledge of the WALL that I feel must keep up because people hurt, they really do. Innuendos deepened the wounds. The impression was given that the family must endure punishment for *allowing* their daughter to be in the wrong place. It causes a tremendous amount of guilt.

My pastor told me, "The murder was somehow part of God's plan. You *must* forgive the young man who killed your daughter."

"The great acts of love are done by those who are habitually performing small acts of kindness."

—*Anonymous*

☎ National Organization of Parents
   of Murdered Children   (513) 721-5683

Part 7

LIFE CHANGES

DIVORCE

Sheila is a vivacious woman in her mid-thirties. She is an advertising agency representative. As soon as one meets her one is drawn by her winning personality.

My divorce will not be final until a couple weeks. It's very new. We were married sixteen years.

The most annoying thing that several people have asked was if I was seeing someone. "Boyfriend?" It makes me angry that people will automatically assume that when a woman leaves a marriage she must be seeing someone on the side. That really bothers me. It's like saying that we are not adult enough to make decisions on what's best for us. It is a very rude assumption. Both sexes make that remark. I was very surprised because that question came also from a fairly good friend. I looked at her thinking, did she really ask me that? I was amazed.

I was talking to a woman explaining the process, telling her I didn't want the divorce to drag on. She replied, "You don't seem to be wasting any time." Like I should let it drag for a year or two and people will suffer more than they need to because that's what people think must be done. As far as I am concerned when a marriage is over there is no point of dragging it out for either party. It needs to be taken care of.

A lot of people ask me, "Why?" Some people I don't mind telling them why. Some others that I don't know well have asked me that question. It seems a bit odd as it is too personal. It's very nervy. I don't know what their circumstances are, whether they are thinking of getting a divorce or what, but it is totally inappropriate. I never know what reaction I am going to get.

Our very best friends don't know. I just didn't want to call and say, "Gosh. I wanted to let you know that..." How do you tell people you have been friends with for a long time? I'll just wait until they call, fill them in that way. I have also been surprised at the support that I have received from very unexpected places. Seems that anyone who has been through a divorce is very supportive. They really understand what's involved in the process, emotionally and legally.

There is a lot of grief with the loss of a relationship. At some point people started saying, "You should get on with it. Get over what you are feeling." Or, "Well, you are the one who made the decision, how can you be grieving this kind of loss?" It is difficult.

I go from feeling really good to feeling very depressed, very sad and all the gambit of emotions. It is a blessing that we don't have children.

It's interesting that for the most part my husband and I have been able to stay on friendly terms. He went through a period of anger, I'll get back at you, but it didn't last. I have been very grateful for that. We have been able to speak without yelling or screaming. That has helped.

What's interesting is the role of the lawyers. I am amazed at how unconcerned they are about how you feel emotionally. The way they drag their feet. It seems that the process is very cold from the legal stand point. It is difficult enough without having to fight the person who is representing you. I would recommend retaining a female lawyer. I really think that it would help.

At work they were supportive as they had seen how unhappy I had been for the past few years. They have seen the difference since we have been separated. I seem so much happier, more content. Several of my co-workers have mentioned that. I really am. But, there is always that one person to pester you with the question, "Have you started dating?" or "You are young, you'll marry again and start a new life." Really!

My relationship with married couples has drastically changed. One couple we ran around with a lot have had interesting reactions. We did a lot of social things together. First they said they wanted to be supportive of both sides. It's fine with me. I wouldn't want them to give up their friendship with my husband because we were getting divorced. It's interesting because they haven't socialized with him or me either. I think it's been very threatening to them, very threatening. Another couple are having their own marital problems. It puts the issue so close in front of them that it's better not to deal with it by avoiding me and him. That has been very interesting but actually surprising. I don't want to put them in an uncomfortable situation. I would be uncomfortable also. I just have to let it go. Quite a twist.

I noticed the change with my customers. My job requires a lot of socializing. Before the divorce it was non-threatening because my husband was with me. Now it is very threatening to the wives as most of my customers are men and they bring their wives and I am *single*. It has created a little tension in several situations. I have done nothing but try to be gracious to the wives in front of the husbands.

At a training conference my supervisor told me that since I was going to be divorced I would have extra time and could work longer hours. That really angered me. Because it is an assumption that I am not going to have a life now. Wait a second! I still socialize, I still have activities, I still have things I need to do in the house. I am not going to spend all of my time working. After her divorce all my boss did was *work*.

I should not have to figure out why people say strange things.

I was very nervous about telling my parents because we had been married so long. They love Bob like a son. They wanted to come for the long Thanksgiving weekend. I called them to make them aware of the situation. I told them, "Bob and I are separated and we are going to be divorced. If you can't be supportive of me while you are here, I would prefer that you stay home. I need all the support I can get right now." They amazed me, they were wonderful. My dad in particular was a total surprise. Since then he has called me a couple of times to see how I am doing. He never did that before. So, it actually brought us closer together.

I started going for counseling. It has helped tremendously to sort through things because at times I don't know what I am feeling for sure. I don't know whether it's anger, I am afraid, or just sad. I would recommend counseling for everyone going through a divorce. What am I going to do? There are going to be a lot of changes coming up. Opportunities to do some things I might not have had the chance to do before being married. It's a very confusing kind of situation. I feel some guilt. I would like to go in the direction of creative things. When I got married it was put on the back burner. I like photography, and playing the piano. I took more than ten years of piano lessons. I want to make sure that I use this time to find out who I am, what I am all about, get to know myself a lot better. I have time to do that, it's scary, but interesting. It's also full of surprises. Finding out what is important to me as a person and what my needs and wants are. It's been a challenge. Lots of new things can be done, now it's finding the courage to do it.

"You never really understand a person until you consider things from his point of view."

—Harper Lee, To Kill a Mockingbird

☎ For support groups, consult listing in local telephone directory

PREGNANCY

Jennifer is a secretary in a large investment office. She is tall with beautiful long, blond hair.

One day, all excited, during a coffee break I gave my co-workers the news of my first pregnancy. I was showered with congratulations and good wishes except by one person. This woman started to tell me all the things that could go wrong during a pregnancy, citing all kinds of examples of women she knew who had miscarriages, gave birth to a Down Syndrome child, retarded or deformed children. She went on and on, the list was endless until someone had the presence of mind to take that woman aside, give her a good scolding and tell her to keep her mouth shut.

When you are pregnant, the worst platitudes are told by health care providers. They treat you as if you are ill. You are healthy, well, and feeling wonderful.

Every time I went to the doctor it seemed he always had some new thing for me to worry about. Keep in mind that I had a trouble-free pregnancy; there was nothing to worry about. He often made me feel anxious when I didn't need to be.

Most people thought that my husband and I were not going to have children because we had told them that we were not planning a family. The main reason was that it was easier as people tend to bug you asking, "When are you going to have kids?"

When I found out that I was pregnant and I told a friend the wonderful news, she said, "Is that good or bad? Well, you can do something about it if it is not what you want."

Because my ankles were swollen I went to see the nurse practitioner. She asked if I ate excessively salty food. "I don't think so," was my answer.

"Did you eat Mexican food?"

"Yes."

"Ham?"

"Yes."

Her kind answer was, "You deserve having swollen ankles!"

My reaction was not good because during my pregnancy my first concern was the baby. I was extremely careful not to harm the baby in any way. Maybe I was overly sensitive, but she should have realized that it was not an appropriate way to tease. Still it was good that she was advising me what food to avoid. But the nurse could have instead said, "Have you considered cutting down on salty foods?" I would have answered, "I will." It would have been a more positive experience.

When I was four months pregnant a friend exclaimed,
"Oh! You look so big."

We want to look pregnant but not be told that we are
so big.

A very common phenomenon, not often talked about,
is losing the physical barrier around yourself, your privacy.
People put their hands on your body, pat your tummy
asking, "How is the baby doing?"[1]

It didn't bother me that much because I was excited
and so happy to be pregnant for the first time. But, it
makes a lot of women uncomfortable.

People think they can do it because we've changed and
it is acceptable if you're pregnant.

Most people were wonderful. Never had so many
incredible friends told me how happy they were for me.
They were all sweet and kind. "What can I do for you?"
they would ask. I was given incredible baby showers.

After the birth of my little boy, a woman told me, "I
don't understand why you chose to have a natural way of
giving birth when you could have taken advantage of
modern medicine." She was making an evaluation on how
my baby should be born, without knowledge of *my* wishes.
She felt her way was superior.

One of the things I learned from talking to a lot of
pregnant women is everybody has her own ideas about the
right way of giving birth. It goes from wanting no medi-

---

[1] **Author's note:** Ordinarily, we don't go around touching
people's tummies! If we would like to do so, permission should
be asked first.

cation all the way to knock-me-out-at-the-first-sign-of-pain, which is not an option these days. It is inappropriate for any of us to make assessments of others. Also asking in advance, "What are you planning to do?" is fine only if it's genuine interest, not evaluation. If you choose to have a natural birth, that is a personal decision. People say, "Why, when you can have drugs?" Why would I have drugs? I felt they would be bad for my baby. I had very strong feelings on the way I wanted it to happen *for me*, but I learned an important message that other people have different ideas. Every woman is entitled to have her baby the way she wants to have it.

After the birth of the baby, another issue popped up. How to raise my child!

When the baby cries, "Aren't you going to pick it up?" or "You aren't going to pick him up are you? You are going to spoil him," or "You are letting the baby sleep in the bed with you? That's really strange."

There has been a lot of research on the best way to raise children. Wouldn't it be better for one woman to say to another, "This is the way I raised my children. I don't know what you want to do, but these are the things I've tried that you might want to consider."

After my beautiful boy was born, the subject of circumcision turned up. I discussed it with many professionals as well as close friends. My aunt totally surprised me by saying, "Whatever it says in the Bible, that's what you are supposed to do." For certain faiths that's appropriate, but my family is not Jewish. I was amazed by her response.

Many people have misconceptions about circumcision. People told me to have it done because when my son went to school, he would be embarrassed in gym class because he was not circumcised and different.

After her baby was born, another friend went to a maternity store to purchase a nursing brassiere. It is usually recommended that you wait until your milk is coming in so you'll know the proper size.

Looking up the clerk said, "When are you due?" My friend had had the baby a week before. She didn't take that remark very well, especially in a maternity store.

After my son's second birthday, a friend started to ask me, "When are you going to have a baby brother or sister for your child?"

It was really none of her business. The question is especially rude to women who have a hard time getting pregnant. How in the world do you respond? It is no one's business if a couple has been trying and hasn't been able to conceive. For some women, it is a very sensitive issue. A better way if one has to ask might be, "Do you plan to have more children?" instead of "Why don't you have more children?"

When I am annoyed by others' inquisitiveness I answer, "No, the one I have is perfect."

Be careful of giving advice.
Wise men don't need it
and
fools won't heed it.

—Meg Branquet

PARENTING

Casual and hurtful remarks can have long lasting effect on children.

After catching me whistling, which was often the case, my Maman would repeatedly tell me, *"Les petites filles ne sifLent pas. Tu fais pleurer la Sainte Vierge."* (Little girls don't whistle. You are making the Holy Virgin Mary cry.) At that young age it was beyond my comprehension why Mary would cry. I realized later that Maman was trying with little success to make a lady out of me.

Being compared to my older sister created opposite reactions. "Why can't you behave like her?" I didn't want to, I wanted to be me. I rebelled.

When a teenager, I was all legs and arms. My brother, who was eleven years older used to tell me that men didn't marry women with ugly legs. I have been hiding them ever since under slacks.

The most powerful and hurtful words from my mother to her tomboy daughter were, "What did I do to God to

have a daughter like you. I'll never be able to marry you!"
It had such a profound effect that I married the first man
who asked me. Very long lasting powerful words. To
another teenager, "You are not going to wear this skirt,
are you? You don't have the best legs in the world."
When we say unkind things to children, we damage
their self-image.

You are pathetic.
You mess up everything you start.
You have crooked teeth. Don't smile. It looks terrible.
You disgust me.
You disappoint me.
You can't do anything right.
Shut up!
Hey stupid! Don't you know how to listen?
You are more trouble than you are worth.
I am sick of looking at you.
I wish you were never born!
You are useless.
Don't be silly!
Quit acting like a child!
You never care about anyone but yourself, you are
  selfish.
You are always whining.
What are you always complaining about?
If you misbehave, I am not going to love you anymore.
Grandma will have a heart attack.
Mom will start drinking again.

Such remarks become deeply embedded bruises which
stay in a child's heart. Many children have carried the

burden of a parent's thoughtless remark with them through adulthood.

"The sweetest sound of all is praise."

—Xenophon

"Sincere praise reassures children. It helps them neutralize doubts they have about themselves."

—Anonymous

"So many gods, so many creeds, so many paths that wind and wind,
While just the art of being kind is all the sad world needs."

—Anonymous

Part 8

THE LANGUAGE

HAVE YOU HURT ANYONE WITH WORDS TODAY?

"Good words cost nothing, but are worth much."

—Unknown

Can we go for twenty-four hours without saying an unkind word? Which ones are *your* top 10 clichés?

1. It's not all that bad.
2. It could be worse.
3. I know how you feel.
4. I understand.
5. Get over it.
6. It's not a big deal.
7. You have to be grateful.
8. Just forgive.
9. It happened a long time ago—forget it!
10. Time heals all wounds.

Over and over and over Again!

It could be worse.

You'll feel better tomorrow.

No big deal.

Time heals all wounds.

You'll get over it.

I know how you feel.

Forget it.

I understand.

Others are worse off.

Put it behind you.

Get on with your life. Stop moping.
Put it behind you.
You have to get on with your life
You need to work through it.
It can't get any worse.
Look at the bright side.
You are going to feel better tomorrow.
Tomorrow will be a better day.
Be patient.
You'll get over it.

Engage Brain Before Speaking

Put it out of your mind.
Better days are coming.
Many people are worse off than you are.
No pain, no gain.
Everything will be all right.
Put it out of your mind.
Move on.
Cheer up!
Chin up!
Snap out of it!
Don't be sad!

If we are sad, we need a kind person to listen. The above clichés weigh us down. Repressing our feelings can create additional stress. It can be deadly and destructive.

"I don't want them to decide how I am going to act."
—*John Powell, S.J. "Why am I afraid to tell you who I am?"*

You *should* forgive (more of a matter of letting go).

"Before we can forgive one another, we have to understand one another."

—*Emma Goldman*

It's God's will.
It's your cross to bear.
God doesn't send any more than one can stand!

These statements, meant to acknowledge the religious source of comfort have become clichés filled with admonition.

Then why do people crack under unbearable stress? Again, we don't help by deciding when someone else's Higher Power hands out pain and suffering. Such glib remarks push people to the edge of their endurance.

"To judge the responsibility of another is playing God."
—John Powell, S. J. *"Why am I afraid to tell you who I am?"*

If someone were to pay you ten cents for every kind word you spoke today and collect five cents for every unkind word, would you be richer or poorer?

Take a sheet of paper, test yourself. List the kind words that you usually say on one side, and the unkind words and clichés on the other side.

How many of the above clichés have you recently used?

Are you richer or poorer?

ENGAGE BRAIN BEFORE SPEAKING

SMOKE SCREEN FOR CLICHÉS

That's just the way I am.
I can't help myself!
I just lost control.
It runs in the family.
I don't have the willpower to change.
One day I will change.
What ever will be will be.
That does not bother me.
I was overcome with passion.
I didn't mean to hurt you.
I was drinking.
The alcohol made me do it.
I will be happy when...
Why can't I be as lucky as..?
What's the big deal, everyone else is doing it.
I was only kidding.

The above represent the type of thinking that keeps our lives revolving in small circles. Such assumptions contribute to a recurrence of past mistakes and keep our lives at a standstill.

Unfortunately society excuses offenders who disregard people's feelings with more clichés:

They didn't know what to say.
They didn't mean it.
They meant well!
They didn't mean to hurt.
Boys will be boys.
That's the way people are.
That's the way men are.

Why excuse unkind words when they *do* hurt!

"I am sorry." Apologies are shallow if meant to absolve wrongdoing, allowing us to avoid giving it another thought. Sincere apologies are not always easy, but entail thinking and soul searching. Empty apologies are addictive precisely because they excuse thoughtlessness.

Why is it that when we have a serious sickness or accident we ask, "Why me?"

Did we ever hear a person ask when something good happens, "Why me?"

"Kindness is the oil that takes the friction out of life."
—*Unknown*

WHERE DID CIVILITY and CARING GO?

"*The music that can deepest reach, and cure all ill, is cordial speech.*"

—*Ralph Waldo Emerson*

"*Good manners will open doors that the best of education cannot.*"

—*Unknown*

Manners used to be *in*, now they are *out*. Courtesy is not cool!

Have the words, *thank you, you are welcome, please, would you mind, excuse me* disappeared from our vocabulary? Where did these words go?

Our society is experiencing an explosion of incivility. RUDE people are taking over. We run into them from the highways to the telephone.

At a stop light, a man rolled down his window, yelled "Are you stupid? Don't you know how to use turn signals?" followed by four letter words. Even as he was driving away he was still cursing and using obscene gestures.

Foul language is everywhere in the media, movies, sports. We are all saturated.

In elevators people push in and out like hockey players attempting to score.

In the business world one seldom talks to a live person. One is connected to a voice box. A sugary voice recites similar messages, "I am away from my desk or with a customer, please leave your name and telephone number and your call will be returned as soon as possible."

Most of the time the call is not returned. No sense calling again to listen to the same message and be ready in exasperation to throw the telephone through the window.

In these days of automation, calling agencies for information or help is, most of the time, a nightmare. "List of options. To talk to our accounts payable, press 1, bookkeeper press 2. One presses 2, wrong department. Try again. The second time after pressing all the options, none seem applicable. Also be *careful*, if selections are not made within the allotted time, the sugary, nasal, impersonal voice takes you to task. "Your entry is not recognized, try again!" Do we have the strength to start all over again or have we forgotten why we called?

What happened to the pleasure of hearing a business telephone operator say, "Real Paper Company. May I help you?"

"I would like to speak to Mr. Papermill."

"His line is busy. Would you hold, please."

"Yes, I will. Thank you."

What welcome silence... No intrusive background music or sales pitch.

Shortly after a business voice, "Papermill here. What can I do for you?"

A live person!

What happened to department store sales clerks who had time to help customers select clothes. Due to downsizing, they are too busy doing something else. Some of the newer breed boringly will answer your question about some merchandise,

"Everything is on the floor. If you don't find what you want, we don't have it."

No longer calling if another store has the item you wish to purchase or even checking the stockroom. Still one encounters many pleasant ones.

Isn't it annoying to have an item picked, and no cashier is available. Walking around with your purchase wanting to scream, "I want to pay. Please, someone take my money."

When anger overcomes us, we need to restrain our tongues carefully.

Cordial speech brings smiles.

Any good, therefore, that I can do or any kindness I can show to any fellow creature, let me do it now.

Let me not defer or neglect it.

For I shall not pass this way again.

—Etienne de Grellet

UNCARING and UNCIVILIZED SPEECH

Coarseness of speech, rudeness, sarcasm (tearing flesh in Greek), sadism, tell it like it is. We can also hurt with mockery, body and eye language.

A woman prided herself in being always truthful — an excuse to say anything she wanted to say. She is malevolent.

After a hysterectomy her doctor told a woman, "So what, you have three children."

To a neighbor who has laryngitis, "It's because you talk too much!"

When an author received a call from the biggest bookstore in Chicago, his friend said, "How in the world did they hear about *you*?"

A woman was invited to a very important community meeting. An acquaintance passing by her seat, stopped and said, "What are *you* doing here?" Another time she told another friend that she was asked to address a university class.

"Why would they would want *you*?"

At a party, a man knowing that one of the guests was born in France made the following remark, "Forty-two percent of French people are illiterate, and I can't stand their body odor."

Two women talking, one's husband comes in. After he left, the other woman said, "I only look at good looking men."

A real estate woman presented her realtor with an important contract. He turned to a colleague, "Another woman taking off her apron to see if she can do it."

A woman called her mother to tell her that she was in the hospital, "Why does everything happen to me?" exclaimed the mother.

We can restore civility in our society by starting with ourselves. Civility can be contagious. Start with little acts, you'll be surprised at the change in yourself and people you come in contact with.

In a grocery store a young man behind the delicatessen counter was pleasantly chatting with a customer while completing her order. The next customer told him, "Young man, I like your personality. Keep it up."

The smile on his face was worth the little compliment. He will remember.

Why don't we all sing?

"Eliminate the negative and accentuate the positive?"

> *Drop a pebble in the water,*
> *And it's ripples reach out far;*

And the sunbeams dancing on them
May reflect them to a star.
Give a smile to someone passing,
Thereby making morning glad;
It may greet you in the evening
When your own heart may be sad.
Do a deed of simple kindness;
Though it's end you may not see,
It may reach like widening ripples
Down a long eternity.

From a little book of poems published
by Salesian Missions, New York

ENGAGE BRAIN BEFORE SPEAKING

EPILOGUE

"To look directly into the face of humanity and not turn away is perhaps the greatest thing one man can do to another."

—*Albert Camus*

It's when we are uncomfortable with someone else's pain that we say words irresponsibly. *ENGAGE BRAIN BEFORE SPEAKING* was written to help readers be more aware of what they say to others. When we have problems, we are not ourselves, kind words go a long way. Courtesy and warm interest in others can work miracles.

In many communities neighbors remain strangers. We need to rebuild a civil society which treats people as if they matter. Politeness is how we treat and deal with each other positively.

Usage of good words can be learned from the interviews contained in this book, and from other publications and poems on caring which expound on the usage of soothing and healing words. The people interviewed for *ENGAGE BRAIN BEFORE SPEAKING* show clearly how intimately they have been hurt by people's lack of understanding and compassion. How poorly considered words, attitudes, lack of caring effected their lives. Their stories have a common link: they are all recipients of hurtful clichés.

Many comments seem innocent enough until we actually stop and think about their meaning and impact. Insensitive clichés, words and remarks have the power to devastate. Sometimes the worst offenders are people near and dearest to us. While families provide refuge from the outside world, the closeness seems to give permission to abandon the niceties that make the world an easier place to live.

"The beginning of love is to let those we love be perfectly themselves, and not to twist them to fit our image. Otherwise we love only the reflection of ourselves we find in them."

—Thomas Merton (No man is an island)

By saying, "It's a matter of *will power*," we judge the addicted. As simple as it sounds, this cliché discounts the underlying causes of addictions by saying it's all a matter of a character flaw. Perhaps we can admit how little we know about addictions and self-help groups as Alcoholic Anonymous, Gamblers Anonymous, Narcotic Anonymous and Overeaters Anonymous. Why not merely rejoice with them for their courage and perseverance in living one day at a time.

We can say, "I am so glad you are doing so well. It can't be easy."

How sad that Liz and Bob are discriminated against because of their disorders. It's easy to make fun of people who don't fit the image commonly expected. Calling them weirdos is senseless and unkind. We should admire them for their courage in leading their lives as constructively and fully as possible.

"God wove a web of loveliness, of clouds and stars and birds, but made not anything at all so beautiful as words."

—*Anna Hempstead Branch*

Again we can say, "I am so glad you are doing so well. It can't be easy."

Roberta, mother of the severely handicapped child, reminds us that her child is a *human being.* The hearing, visually impaired and the wheelchair user don't want to be treated in a condescending manner. They are people first, people who happen to have impairments.

"Words have weight, some are heavy others are light. Before we use them they need to be measured."

—*Meg Branquet*

It seems that the bereaved are overwhelmed with *HAVE TO, YOU SHOULD* and *PUT IT BEYOND YOU.* As the interviews reveal, what people need most in any crisis are listeners. It's important to remember that they are fragile. They need friends who can remain available. After the funeral we can offer practical help. Phone calls and kind notes can follow. While visiting we

· can say, "Since your loss my thoughts have been with you, and I wanted to tell you in person."

"You must miss him/her terribly."
"How difficult it must be to have your best friend so sick."
"It must be hard to no longer have your mother near you. You were so devoted to her."

"I would like to give you some of my strength while you are down."

—Meg Branquet

Society makes a fetish of fitness which causes people to turn away from anyone who doesn't fit the perfection mold. Outward appearances can often be misleading. The sick don't necessarily *look sick*. Everyone wants to be treated with dignity and encouraging words.

"Let a good person do good deeds with the same zeal that an evil person does bad ones."

—Shalom Rokeach

We can't fix suffering, so why do we think we can and that we *have to* say something?

"I don't know what to say" is one of the most helpful comments because it is truthful. "May I give you a hug?" if accepted can do wonders.

A sincere note stating, "I want you to know that I am thinking of you," will be helpful.

Recipe: A generous portion of kindness, mix well with a tablespoon of wisdom.

We owe people the courtesy of being kind and, most of all, thoughtful.

Instead of giving me hope,
You gave me scorn.
Instead of a helping hand,
You gave me advice.
Instead of listening,
You drowned me in shoulds.
Instead of understanding,
You gave me doubt.

—Meg Branquet

Past the seeker as he prayed, came the crippled, the beggar and the beaten. Seeing them the holy one went down on his knees into deep prayer, "Great God, how is it that a loving creator can see such things and yet do nothing about them?"

After a long silence, God said,

"I did do something. I sent you."

—Sufi teaching story (paraphrased)

ENGAGE BRAIN BEFORE SPEAKING

RESOURCES

ADDICTIONS

☎ Alcoholic Anonymous	(212) 685-1110
☎ Al-Anon (Family/friends of alcoholics)	(800) 356-9996
☎ Narcotics Anonymous	(800) 352-3792
☎ Overeaters Anonymous	(505) 891-2664

SICKNESSES

☎ AIDS hotline	(800) 342-2437
☎ Alzheimer's Association	(800) 272-3900
☎ American Cancer Society	(800) ACS-2345
☎ Arthritis	(800) 283-7800
☎ Epilepsy Society of America	(800) EFA-1000
☎ Lupus Foundation of America	(800) 558-0121
☎ National Heart Association	(314) 373-6300
☎ National Multiple Sclerosis Foundation	(212) 986-3240
☎ United Cerebral Palsy	(800) 872-5827

continued

PHYSICALLY IMPAIRED

☎ National Association of the Deaf   (301) 587-1788
                      TDDY (301) 587-1789
☎ The Lighthouse, Inc.   (800) 334-5497

GRIEF

☎ AARP Widowed Persons Service   (202) 434-2260
☎ Compassionate Friends National Office
  (for parents who have lost a child) (708) 990-0010

☎ MADD (Mothers Against
  Drunk Drivers)   (800) 438-6233
☎ American Association of
  Suicidiology   (202) 237-2280
☎ SA/VE Suicide Awareness/
  Voices of Education   (612) 946-7998

VIOLENCE

☎ Against Our Will peer support group
  for sexual assault survivors   (518) 434-0439
☎ VOICES in Action, Inc. (Victims Of
  Incest Can Emerge Survivors)   (312) 327-1500
☎ Domestic Violence   (800) 333-7230
                      TDD (800) 787-3224
☎ Family Violence Prevention Fund (800) 313-1310
☎ National Coalition Against
  Domestic Violence   (303) 839-1852
☎ National Crime Victim Center   (703) 276-2880
☎ National Organization of Parents
  of Murdered Children   (513) 721-5683
☎ NOVA (National Organization
  for Victim Assistance)   (202) 232-6682

☎ Children of Aging Parents (800) 227-7294
☎ Eldercare Locator (helps caregivers
locate local services for the aging) (800) 677-1116
☎ National Center for Elder Abuse (202) 682-0100
☎ National Senior Citizens Law
Center (202) 887-5280
☎ AARP Consumers Affairs (202) 434-2277
☎ National Fraud Information Center (800) 876-7060

Publications

For Caregivers

📖 *Caretakers, the Forgotten People* (800) 848-1192
Maita Floyd
📖 "A Path for Caregivers" (D12957)
AARP, 601 E St., NW Washington, DC 20049

ABOUT THE AUTHOR

After a thirty-year airline career Maita Floyd retired in the Ahwatukee community of Phoenix, Arizona. Her writing career started after her husband's death in 1987. Besides writing she devotes much of her time to community service: Maricopa county district attorney victim/witness advocate and hospice volunteer. Maita is a member of the Arizona Governor's Commission on Violence Against Women Task Force.

For Tremendous Contributions of Unit Volunteerism, Maita received the 1995-1996 American Legion Auxiliary Western Region Community Service National Award and one of the top three 1996 Interstate Community Foundation, ICF Volunteers of the Year Program.

Maita represented Arizona as a Congressional Senior Citizen Intern in Washington, D.C.

Member of the Arizona Authors' Association, American Business Women Association (1996 fall magazine member profile).

For her role during WWII as a courier in a French/Basque underground escape route, Maita had the great honor of becoming a member of the United States Special Forces and *friend* member of the Air Forces Escape & Evasion Society.

She was awarded an honorary membership with The American Academy of Experts in Traumatic Stress, recognizing a commitment to the advancement of intervention for survivors of trauma.

Maita has been interviewed on television and radio. She lectures nationally on the topics of her books.

A talented artist, Maita can often be found in front of her easel. She finds time to enjoy her favorite sport of tennis.

Order Form

☐ Yes! Please send me *Engage Brain Before Speaking* plus these other books by Maita Floyd.

Name _____

Address _____

City _____ State ____ Zip _____

Phone _____

Book Title	Qty.	Cost Ea.	Total
Engage Brain Before Speaking	____	$10.95	____
Stolen Years *in my little corner of the world*	____	$12.95	____
Caretakers, *the Forgotten People*	____	$ 9.95	____

Shipping:	
1 book	$2.00
2 to 3 books	$3.00
4 books	$4.00

Sub-total ____

Shipping ____

TOTAL $ ____

Mail order make check payable to:
  Eskualdun Publishers Ltd.
  P.O. Box 50266
  Phoenix, AZ 85076-0266
Visa and MasterCard accepted

Card # _ _ _ _ _ _ _ _ _ _ _ _ _ _ _ _   Exp date _ _ / _ _

To order by phone call 1-800-848-1192.
In Arizona, call (602) 893-2394 or
fax (602) 893-9225 or email eskuald@azbz.com